Deliverance: Birth of a Prophet

Uncontrolled Premonitions: A Spiritual Memoir of Visions, Dreams, and Revelations

Wade J. Bell

This book is presented as a personal account drawn from the author's experiences, reflections, dreams, and spiritual interpretations. It is offered for informational, inspirational, and literary purposes.

Published by T.U.E. Publishing Group

A Titan Universe brand

Deliverance: Birth of a Prophet

Uncontrolled Premonitions: A Spiritual Memoir of Visions, Dreams, and Revelations

Based on actual experiences

First Edition

Author's Note

This book is drawn from experiences I have had over many years through dreams, premonitions, spiritual impressions, and visionary encounters. Some sections are presented as I experienced or received them, including narrative sequences, symbolic scenes, and voices that came to me with unusual clarity.

I do not ask the reader to agree with every interpretation in these pages. I only ask that you read with openness and understand that this work is offered as a record of what I have lived, seen, felt, and struggled to understand.

Some passages are deeply personal. Others are spiritual, symbolic, and cosmic in scale. Together, they form the language through which these experiences came to me. Whether you approach this book through faith, curiosity, skepticism, or personal searching, my hope is that you will read it with patience, reflection, and an open mind.

Prologue

For most of my life, I have experienced vivid dreams, premonitions, and spiritual encounters that I could not easily explain or ignore. Some came as warnings. Some came as revelations. Some unfolded like living narratives while I slept, only to remain with me long after I woke. This book is my attempt to document those experiences as honestly as I can.

What follows is not written to force belief or to argue against every religious or scientific explanation of reality. It is written because these experiences were real to me, persistent, and impossible to dismiss. They shaped the way I understand dreams, purpose, creation, fear, faith, and the unseen.

For years, I have carried these experiences privately, trying to make sense of what I was seeing and why I was seeing it. At times they were unsettling. At times they were overwhelming. At times they felt like fragments of a larger truth that I was being asked to witness before I was ready to understand it. This book reflects that journey.

Some readers may view these pages as spiritual testimony. Others may see them as visionary experience, symbolic revelation, or deeply personal reflection. However they are received, they are presented here as truthfully as I can tell them. I only ask one thing of you before you continue: read with an open mind.

What you are about to read comes from years of experiences that stayed with me, challenged me, and refused to let me go. Most came while I was asleep. All of them left an imprint on my life.

This is the record of uncontrolled premonitions.

Chapter 1: It Is... A...

I would start this off by saying "In the beginning I created Heaven and Earth" which you already know, but that would easily deny the one question that all of my creations have had at one point in their existence. That question happens to be, "What happened before I created Heaven and the Earth? Well, I will discuss that topic after I say this. In case you didn't know or don't remember, everything and everyone was created in my likeness or image. This should automatically tell you that your thoughts and ideas are never wrong. I gave you the power to think and choose. It's your actions and spoken words that makes you whole or condemns your soul. This is where Satan plays a prominent role. However, you'll learn this soon enough. Now it's time to help answer that question you have, Wajolebe.

Before there were angels, and a Heaven and an Earth, there was just I and nothing more. I know you may ask yourself how I got here if there was nothing, or do I have parents. Well, even I am too complex to explain, but I will help you understand. First, try imagining the Ultimate. Sure, this is what I am, but this is not easy for you to comprehend. Instead, for your conception, try imagining purgatory or a complete emptiness with no sound or no such thing as time. You just are and there just is. Nothing ever changes, not even you. Now don't take this example the wrong way. Trust me; I know your heart, Wajolebe. It's telling you right now that purgatory is a terrible comparison, but what you need to remember is that I'm only describing this for your contentment. But just in case, I'll help you understand me in a different way. So let's continue forward.

Think back to a time where you reached the peak of exhaustion, but you can't go to sleep because it's important that you stay awake for whatever reason. Now instantly skip yourself to the part where your friends wake you from a deep sleep. You probably won't believe that you were asleep until you notice that two or three hours have passed.

During that time, the only things that you had while asleep were your thoughts. Time passed for your friends, but it didn't seem to pass for you at all until your waking period. That unknown elapse period that I speak of is where I began, and all that I had where my thoughts as well. There were many of them that passed, but only one that lingered. "I need love" was that specific one. My need is simple, yet so hard to understand and acquire. I need to give love as well as receive it. With just one thought or breath, I could've easily changed that to accommodate my need, but what's to accommodate if there's nothing to give? Love cannot be forced. For that's what makes love eternal. I know your heart, and it's telling me that you understand me now, Wajolebe. So you should relax because I'm about to tell you the story of what happened before the Heaven and Earth that you know of existed. I will become the narrator, but I will be as myself. Take notes, Wajolebe.

As the many thoughts pass, I reach a conclusion to devise a perfect plan that would turn this nothingness to something and spread the love that's undoubtedly needed throughout by creating. "This plan will express my undying love for all creations," it thinks while putting the perfect plan into motion. "Let there be time," I, Alpha, speak for the first time breaking the barrier of this complete emptiness. A thunderous sound emits within this nothingness and continuously spreads with an unstoppable and immeasurable force, stretching nothing into an unoccupied space perpetually. This moment manifests the beginning of time of just It; I; Alpha. Now that I have spoken, there are other elements of my plan that need to exist. Witnesses are required to verify the wondrous glory of my plan, and to love all of time, empty space, and everything soon to be within. So with a single thought, "Let the spirit become," spirits are created one by one, but they have no names at this point. There are so many created that it would be humanly impossible to count; yet they each have something unique about them.

So, I begin to speak again, but this time through thought transference because one sound of my voice could destroy everything quicker than I created it. This is how I will speak from now until the end of time. "I am It, the answer to all, Alpha, the Almighty, and the Creator. No spirit shall be granted the Will, but you shall be granted eternal life and love by my side. Will is in the eye of the beholder. You all will be assigned a name, and it will be your gift and duty to carry out. You will have questions, but don't worry because all questions will be answered when asked. With that said, witness the joyous wonders that I'm going to overwhelm you with," I smile magnificently while extending both my arms.

"I will have two sons. The first will be called Lucifer who shall be known as the morning star, the highest ranking, and the leader of my army. The second will be called Michael who shall be known as the savior. You shall be called Gabriel, my personal messenger. And you will be called Raphael the healer, and the bringer of joy and love. Uriel, the angel of salvation, come forth. Israfel, the angel of song will be your name. Uzziel, you will be known as the angel of mercy. Come forth Azrael, Fannel, Sariel, Jeremiel, and Raguel," I continue until every angel is named. They each undeniably welcome the love that surrounds this empty space as an infant embraced by a mother's hug. Each spirit instantly concedes an understanding from the plan that I devised, and since they were all named now, I needed to build a home for them to dwell in.

So, I begin to speak again, "I will now create sovereignty and a place for all to be welcomed. I shall call it Himil, the home and kingdom of, and I shall have a throne to sit upon," I speak while creating this beautiful and magnificent place. All spirits mumble in awee at this extraordinary sight of the most untainted elements and songs of life. "I shall now breathe a heaven, and Himil will be the kingdom of it. You'll also witness this phenomenon as galaxies and planets suit and fill this empty space with life and love," I say while turning and pointing towards the emptiness. At this moment I breathe an unimaginable fire causing a colossal explosion of dust and life. An explosion that if transpired again would destroy the heavens in a matter of terra seconds. This bang, sequentially, creates a current called the "Breath of Life" rippling and scattering dust throughout space uncontrollably. As the ripples continue to expand, I strategically connect each piece of dust like a jigsaw puzzle to form galaxies. These galaxies are given names, and every name has a gift. This process takes millions and millions of years to complete in your eyes, but only a few moments in mine. Next, I begin to form and name a vast number of planets from this dust, and they too have separate gifts.

"For the names I have just given, this set of spirits shall have a governing responsibility," I say as I select a group of angels based on their gifts to undertake this new task. "These names and your names are linked as one. However, there is one place that I have yet to create that will be the key to my plan. This will be left unaided. Only I shall have overall authority over it," I say as I point to the spot where it will be placed. Every spirit understands their purpose, and without asking a single question, takes their place and waits for the moment to be called upon. Many of the other spirits stand by my side with their own specially assigned gifts; however, all are loved equally with a place beside the throne. At this point in time I have not created light as you know of, but there is a spiritual light that shines bright. Only pure spirits are allowed to set eyes on it. The galaxies and planets are still dark matter for now. I only say this because, in time, there will be a...

Chapter 2: A Jealous Soul Turns Deceitful.

As time passes, I flawlessly construct the galaxy, known to you as the Milky Way, in which to place the solution to the perfect plan. Life is placed in precise locations, and the spirits unquestionably take their places with each piece created. There are twelve planets, no such things as moons, and one brightless sun formed at this moment. "I have now assembled the ideal surroundings...," I announce and continue, "...and you shall now witness the key." Starting the process of forming Eden, the thirteenth planet that will accommodate my final creations, I use very intricate details beginning with the core and moving outward. Still, there is no visible light to accompany time and space because everything has to be in position before I call upon it.

Meanwhile as time passes and I continue to create life throughout the galaxy including calculated locations within the rest of this new universe, the spirits anxiously wait to perform their tasks. "Isn't it lovely that we have the opportunity to witness this creation," asks one angel? "Yes, it is. We have the love of all creations, but to give that love feels even more astounding. Alpha said this would be perfect and it is. It's spectacular," says another as Gabriel makes an entrance. "It most certainly is," replies Gabriel. "And Alpha sends me to say that Eden is nearly complete (simply specifying the world with nothing in it), and the key to this plan will thereafter be unraveled. All questions for now should be answered," Gabriel continues as Lucifer and Michael appear like a gust of wind.

"Ah Lucifer, Michael, one love," Gabriel says. Lucifer nods as Michael raises and lowers his right hand in return. "Did you obtain the message I presently delivered from the Almighty," asks Gabriel? "Yes," replies Michael as they all turned towards Lucifer. Lucifer kindly replies, "I too acquired the message, Gabriel. Thank you for the joyous news. I also overheard you speak that all questions were answered. Did the Almighty also inquire you to speak this," he asks inquisitively at the same time noticing that some of the others were interested also? Gabriel replies by reemphasizing what Alpha had spoken, "Yes. Remember, 'Have no questions because as I speak I shall provide all answers'." Lucifer replies while nodding agreeably, "Yes, yes." However, he does have questions that he feels are unanswered, and it looks as if a few others have questions also. He begins to wonder if Eden will be the last piece of this big plan. It sounds as if something else is going to be added, or maybe he doesn't fully understand the plan and his purpose in it. All in all, this opens up many thoughts in his spirit, which makes him focus on finding an answer.

At this moment he doesn't want to stir up any issues by thinking out loud, so he ventures in spirit. "Shall we prepare the throne for Alpha's return," poses Michael. Every angel rises to the occasion except two. Well of course Gabriel is one, only because he returns the Almighty's word to all creations, not just the angels. Lucifer is the second because he isn't there. Otherwise, he would've also helped prepare the throne.

There are a few things that really have him thinking, so he decides to ask. "Our Father, why did you allow us to think, but not grant us the Will," Lucifer asks curiously? "What exactly is it and why are we not granted it? Why do I have these questions, and am I the only one with them...do the others think like me? I thought the key to your perfect plan was Eden," Lucifer prays while pacing and continues. "However, when Gabriel delivered your message, he said the key will be unraveled afterwards. This sounded as if it was just another piece of your plan. Unless Eden really is the final piece," Lucifer concludes. As quick as he asks these questions, I hear and answer.

"I hear all questions, and I provide all answers. I am one with all spirits my son, and so your questions will be answered as promised. You are not the only one with them, I assure you. You are pure spirit, bodiless, meaning you are born from love. To know of love so pure makes it effortless for you to accept it. You and all spirits have been given this love freely. However, this creates only the first half. Love is known, my son. As of Eden, this will be the second beginning. A seed of life will be planted that will not be of pure spirit, which is the only way to preserve the will. It will preside over all creations on Eden and have full authority. However, with everything provided, a choice will also be given. This is the seed's gift, and with that comes the final piece. Love is believed in and therefore born from faith, my son. It's one thing to know that true love exist, which makes the spirit the strongest foundation, but to choose it by giving and accepting it freely, makes love complete. That's why the Will is useless to possess in true spirit. When you put these two together it finalizes all and becomes absolute. Then I shall exist to all creations as One Love," I reply.

"I understand that everything plays a part in your plan, father, even I. But if you didn't grant us the Will because it's useless to have, then why allow us to think and ask questions," Lucifer asks feeling more confused? "Will is in the eye of the beholder, but only I know the end to all, my son," I respond. Lucifer begins to gradually understand. He sees the purpose of every addition to the plan, and decides that he has no more questions to ask the Almighty. In spirit, on the other hand, he opens up to many more.

He leaves the father to continue the creation of Eden, and secretly from a distance, watches every piece of dust take form. He studies every movement of the spirit and everything that forms thereafter. Slowly he begins to understand the process of creation, how it's executed through his father's eyes, and how simple it is to perform. All things seem to become possible for Lucifer at the time he learns this, which makes him feel as though he can be just as powerful. He witnesses how much time and effort the father is bestowing upon Eden, and starts to feel like the Almighty will favor the future seed more. He starts to believe that the pure spirit may eventually be pushed aside for the seed, or worse, slaves to it. Lucifer can't make any since of these thoughts, so he journeys in spirit to find the answer without disturbing the father again. As time passes, Eden is finally complete. However, it doesn't have any life in it yet; no water, trees, or anything of the sort. For your understanding, it's like a mother's womb without a seed. Yet and still, it's now time to call upon the light because everything is in position, and it's also time for each spirit previously selected to perform their duties as given. "Your duties shall now be fulfilled in spirit. Let there be light for the morning and guiding lights for the night," I declare as each spirit is adorned with the almighty glow.

The spirits wrap their grace around each element of creation, and shines bright to bring all the stars, suns, and planets to light. They are suns during the morning and guiding lights for the night, as requested. The universe is now set in motion. The planets are rotating, suns and stars are shining, and galaxies are spinning. The Milky Way is the only galaxy that remains motionless and the sun constantly shining until the final touches of Eden are completed. Light is specifically called upon to allow all creations the luxury of observing everything created by the Almighty thus far. There is still dark matter scattered throughout time, and has been chosen to remain unseen until warranted. It's unnecessary to call upon it at this moment. Everything is good and this makes the Almighty exultant. Rest is needed, but just enough, in a sense, to weigh the plan of what belongs on Eden. "I shall now rest for an epoch before I create the key," I say while resting upon the throne to contemplate the final portion. Lucifer, on the other hand, is somewhere becoming...

Meanwhile as Alpha rests, Lucifer grows more and more determined to answer every question on his own. Constantly thinking to himself, he's careful not to voice his questions because he doesn't want to disturb the father. "Why was I chosen to lead the army? Why am I the most beautiful out of all the others? No, no, why was I selected as the first and highest ranking? Maybe I'm supposed to rule after the father. No, that's definitely not it. Or is it," Lucifer gives a short pause as he rubs his chin, "...because why did I receive the most? Maybe I'm loved the most," Lucifer thinks hesitantly. "No, that's not it either. We're all loved equally. However, it seems as if more will be offered to this new seed. It will have even more than us...full authority over all creations on Eden...a will to choose...everything,"

Lucifer continues to think while slowly losing focus of the overall plan. "Am I also supposed to have full authority? Am I like this seed? No, because Will is in the eye of the beholder. I mean I have everything that I can possibly gain except the will. If need be, I can even make a seed of my own according to what I've seen father accomplish. Wait...wait...wait...think back...eye of the beholder! What does this mean exactly? We were not granted the Will, but do we still possess it within? Are we just not allowed to use it? We can't possess it because that would defy Alpha's Will. But what if we do?" Lucifer pauses again as if something clicks in spirit. "The father's spirit possesses it and it's pure, and if I remember correctly, no pure spirit will be granted the will," Lucifer thinks as he begins to pace vigorously. "This means the father has falsified the spirit by possessing the will. Can this be true? The Almighty has lied to us. Then this would mean Alpha is not pure. And if the father is impure, then there's weakness within. But this can't be true because why would Alpha lie?"

Lucifer continues to think to himself as he now slowly becomes corrupt with jealousy. "I see. Alpha doesn't want us to know he has weakness. Yeesss!!! Where there is will there's a weakness, and where there's weakness there's a way," as he stops thinking, and speaks out loud. "That's it," Lucifer shouts enthusiastically. "That's the answer. Where there's a will there's a way. Shhhhh," he looks around refusing to be heard and begins to think to himself again. “That’s why the will was not granted to us. Father didn’t want us to become almighty and overthrow the spirit. But that leaves more questions. If will were in the eye of the beholder, then how would I reveal it? Nooo...I get it!! Our love is given freely. So it’s controlled. However, this new seed will have a choice to give and receive it freely. This means that the father’s love will be allowed acceptance or rejection whenever. Once love is not rejected by choice, Alpha will control the unruly and then shall become complete by purifying the true power of the Will through the power of love. There’s nothing else to possess after this. So this will be father’s strength that is now weakness.

The seed is definitely the key to obtaining true and uncontested power,” Lucifer continues to think. As Lucifer becomes fully corrupt by jealousy, he feels as if he’s the only one to make things right. He continues to think, “I need to find out how to create this seed because I can’t allow weakness to rule. The father has the will, which creates weakness. I am without weakness because I am without will. I only need to have authority over it to maintain power. If I could somehow obtain Alpha’s design for this seed then I could gain its love in advance, and render our father powerless. But to do that, I may need some help,” Lucifer says as he begins to ponder.

“Yes, yes...I am the Leader of the Almighty’s army, so I’m pretty sure they will be loyal to me. However, that may become a problem if they are more loyal to the Almighty. Odds are that they will be. My only chance lies in discovering the one’s with similar questions as I. Then I’ll have a better chance of assembling followers by charismatically using everything in my power to persuade them,” Lucifer thinks as he starts to formulate his version of the Perfect Plan. Meanwhile, as Alpha continues to rest and prepare for the new seed, Lucifer continues to decipher a means of stealing it. Now this is a big challenge for him. It’s not like he can sneak up and take it from me, because the whole plan is contained within spirit. But to Lucifer, it's not really a challenge at all due to one fact that he remembers. "Alpha hears all questions, and provides all answers. Exactly...there's no choice but to answer all questions, and I'm going to use this to my advantage," Lucifer imagines as he now embarks on his mission to overthrow the Father and become the Almighty Ruler. "All I need to do is ask questions, but I have to figure out the right ones without divulging my plan," he continuously thinks to himself.

Lucifer paces for a period until he figures out a few questions he wants to ask, however he has to figure out how to ask them. So another period passes until he fathoms this, and then the moment comes to ask. So he journeys back to Himil, bows at the foot of the throne, and speaks, "Our father, I remember how important this new seed is to the achievement of your plan, but if it's not to be of pure spirit, then how will it endure? Will it not have a spirit at all? Will this seed only love you with no knowledge of us, or will we have the opportunity to love it as well. Will it be in the resemblance of us? And Father, will this be the end, or will you have other creations. I only ask this because if the seed is your last creation, then what will be there for it to preside over if no other life exists. I ask these things of you only to perform my duties to the highest degree of your Will," Lucifer asks as he disguises the true reasons behind his intentions.

As promised, I begin to answer his questions, "My son, all questions will be answered. You are already performing your duty as planned, as will all spirits. There will be likeness in spirit of pure and not of pure, which is the spirit combined with the Will. However, this seed will be created in the likeness of I just as you. I have given a piece of my spirit to all foundations, and each piece contains the power within that spirit of creation. The spirit of creation is holy and will be known as such. It always has been and always will be. There will be no difference in the spirit. Although, there will be a temple to house this spirit that will allow it to endure Eden. This temple will contain a soul, which will permit the Will. The seed will have a little knowledge of all creations and a choice to accept them, but there will still be love throughout. I have taken rest my son, because I still have much life to give. The air, water, land, trees, animals...," and so on as I explain a detailed percentage of other creations destined for Eden so that he can have a basic idea of what's in store, "...all of which the seed shall govern. I have yet to choose and number them all, so I shall rest until then. All questions are now answered, and in time, will be," I reply. Lucifer kindly acknowledges the response, and leaves the father, for the final time, to finish resting.

In a sense, Lucifer feels victorious because he believes that he just scammed the Almighty out of this so called Perfect Plan. He knows that even though he's not granted the will, he still has a chance to control it through the seed. All the knowledge that he has gained from the father over the past periods are about to be put to use. "I have it all now; the answers to my questions, the knowledge of all future creations, the plan, and everything else needed. However, I have to use it now without letting the others know. Not yet anyway," Lucifer resorts to thinking again. He figures that if he presently informs the others, the father would likely discover it as well. This is a plan that has to be accomplished privately, and subsequently he will tell the others hoping to convince them. "Given that Eden has previously been formed, I have no desire to reconstruct it...or another. If so, Father will be rested before completion, and I don't possess this amount of time. I will resume from the point where Alpha left off. It'll be much quicker and easier this way," Lucifer says, as jealousy completely takes over his spirit at this point. "If being this way brought this much power to me..."

Chapter 3: Then Greed Brings Forth...

Now, time is definitely not on Lucifer's side seeing that I have already created life so far at an unimaginable rate. The only opportunity available is to intervene during this short period of rest. Lucifer has already mindfully grasped the basic procedures of creation by watching me at work, so this isn't a problem for him. The only negative factor in his equation is time. Perfection and quality are of no significance because there isn't enough time to concentrate on it. The most essential components of his plan are creating, convincing, and freedom.

First, "creating" a foundation worthy of deposing me, this will be referred to as "c". Next, he intends to add "convincing" to the equation, which I'll also refer to as the letter "C". Basically what this means is, he needs to convince whoever has similar questions to accept his thoughts and creations exclusively based on the notion of my Will having fault. These two combined will equal "freedom", which I'll refer to as "F", from my Will allowing the source of pure spirit to inherit Free Will. This is also known as autonomy, sovereignty, or dominion which in turn means more power for Lucifer. C plus c equals f. Remember this equation, Wajolebe. It'll help you later understand one reason why he's associated with the number six. Once he achieves this goal, he wants to be known as the father of it all. However, there are key things that have to be accomplished before his plan will succeed.

First, he has to create the air, water, land, trees, and mostly all the essential things that the Almighty spoke of. Next, he has to make the animals and all things of that sort. And finally, he needs to craft a temple worthy of housing a spirit. These tasks are no problem to perform since he has already factored out perfection and quality. Lucifer continues to ponder, "Even with time against me, I should have no problem accomplishing the first two stages. It's the third that concerns me. Apart from that, I need to get to work in a hurry before father's rest period ends." He journeys out to Eden, swiftly takes pieces of dust and creates life, like he'd previously seen the Almighty execute in other worlds throughout the universe, in the form of air, water, and land. In no time, Lucifer completes stage one. Of course, it isn't a precise construction because he assembled the pieces based on his perception of what Alpha described the blueprint to be.

Nevertheless, he positions the one big land mass in the middle of all the water to place the animals on, and the air above for some animals to fly in. He names the landmass, what you once knew it as, Pangaea. On this newly sculpted island he develops dirt, grass, trees, and all other forms of plant life. Everything is Jurassic an imperfect, but is turning out to be wonderful in his eyes, especially with the time he has to utilize.

"Now for the animals," Lucifer says in a content and imprudent voice as he begins to hastily piece together his conception of the alleged animals previously divulged to him. Again, perfection is not of importance, and upon completion, the animals are far from being precise. For the land animals, some of the bodies are too enormous, but the arms are small. Most of the sea creatures are overly enormous when they should be small. Even the birds created are too enormous and have weird scaly skin. And so far as rationality, none of them have any. But what is done, is done. There is no more time for him to squander on the animals. The most important thing is the seed, and despite the outcome of things he will continue to deliberately defile the Almighty's intentions.

Greed is now prevailing over his spirit at a rapid pace. "Ah, these creations will have to do for now," Lucifer says, as he looks around satisfyingly, and then continues. "At any rate, my goal is nearly complete with only one significant item left, and there's no time to waste. Once I've exiled the Almighty, I'll have all time to reconstruct," Lucifer proclaims as he commences forming the seed, the final portion of the plan. Since this was the key to the Perfect Plan, he visualizes it as close to the Father's vision as possible. Every piece of dust that's collected for the seed is put to use as best as he sees fit. This is unlike the previous creations he molded. Time is actually factored out of this process, and he uses every bit of what time he thinks he has left to create the seed. Upon completion, he smiles agreeably with a haunting grin. He knows that the seed has no life as of yet, and this task is to be delayed until the perfect opportunity. Animating the seed now would probably compromise his situation. In any case, things have to be timed flawlessly from here on out. "I have only one obstacle left to conquer and I shall then overthrow Alpha and be declared the Supreme Being," he proclaims while rubbing his hands together anxiously.

Meanwhile, as Lucifer concludes his treacherous plan, Azrael is at the throne asking similar questions to what Lucifer himself had asked previously. As promised, all questions will be answered. "But father, will this seed know of us, or will you make that a choice for it to know as well...," Azrael questions in a humble voice as Lucifer appears vaguely in the distance behind the wall overflowing with curiosity. "Azrael has the same questions as I. Hmm, I wonder...will he be my first colleague," Lucifer, being careful not to voice any questions, thinks cunningly while chafing his chin. At the same time, Azrael continues to question, "...and will we have the opportunity to share our love with it. I ask these things of you Father only to perform my duties to the highest degree of your Will," he concludes as Lucifer sneers at Azrael's remark, and advances toward the throne. "I can't believe he stole my testimony. He must've been listening in on our conversation from before. Nonetheless, that's exactly who I need on my side," he contemplates and then verbally interrupts the meeting.

"Azrael, these are some of the same questions that I've had in the past, and that the Father answered," Lucifer states as he kneels before the Almighty. "Father, may I have the honor in answering these questions so that you may finish your rest," he asks gallantly. "Lucifer my son, take Azrael's hand and answer his questions as I have done you. Azrael, he shall provide you the knowledge that you seek so that all your questions may be answered," I reply. "In addition Lucifer, I temporarily bestow upon you the power to assist the others with their questions as well. I need complete rest for the final preparation. This power will be returned to me the moment when Gabriel delivers the message to all that I have called on your gifts," I conclude by reaching out and granting Lucifer the power to answer all. Lucifer responds kindly as he turns towards Azrael, "Yes Father. I will proudly do as you order. Come with me Azrael. There's a lot you must know of."

This is all playing into Lucifer's hand easier than what he expects. It's like the whole thing is being placed on a silver platter for him. In any case he takes Azrael by the hand as instructed, and journeys with him a great distance from the Father's throne. During this journey he clarifies all the details that Alpha pointed out including a few of his own. This is all part of the plan, and he's hoping Azrael is naïve to the facts.

"So you're saying that it's all a lie. Basically, Alpha is using us and this so called seed to become Almighty," Azrael asks in a debatable voice. "In the overall sense, yes," Lucifer responds. Azrael paces and then replies, "But how is this so. Everything was created by the hands of the Father, which makes Alpha almighty. And this is so because there was nothing here before the Father. Alpha is the beginning, which makes the foundation almighty," replies Azrael tenaciously. Lucifer feels as though his craftiness slipped right through his hands. He could've sworn that Azrael was the easiest target, however his words were a challenge and they overcame Lucifer for a short moment. But cleverness was becoming his gift, and the time was right for him to use it.

“Follow me and let me demonstrate something for you,” Lucifer gestures and continues. “If the Father is almighty, then by definition that means all powerful. All powerful in turn means creator. There are no questions about this, am I right,” Lucifer asks Azrael in an improper manner? Azrael replies in a confrontational voice, “Yes that is right, so just what are you implying?” Lucifer continues, “What I’m implying is that none of us are creators, more or less have the power to create. As a matter of fact, to animate life is a power only possessed by the father, right,” Lucifer questions Azrael’s intelligence? “Alpha is the only creator with no ifs, ands, or buts about it. We were specifically assigned our own abilities, and none of them are in the realm of the Almighty’s. Are you questioning the father’s intentions, Lucifer? If so, this is blasphemy,” Azrael speaks furiously as Lucifer reaches out to the lifeless seed. “My purpose is not to speak of sacrilege, but of an untold lie,” he replies as he positions his left hand close to his face, and inhales deeply as if he intends to blow a kiss.

Azrael turns in the direction of which Lucifer is pointing, and interrupts abruptly, “What is this I see? Are these the...but how...the father hasn’t created them yet? What are you up to, Lucifer? Answer me. What are trying to prove,” Azrael questions rapidly and then pauses in awe as Lucifer breathes life into the seeds? At the same time he exhales, his spirit becomes full of greed, and darkness distorts his aura. This is unexpected by Lucifer and an astonishment to Azrael, but being exposed in a different light is deemed a small price to pay for supreme power. “I shall name the seeds homan for holy men, and they shall multiply synonymously as the other creations have done thus far. Be fruitful and increase in numbers,” Lucifer speaks as he commands of his creations.

The seeds are awkward as well as the other creations because they were formed in the same manner as the animals, excluding the use of a little more time. They are very hairy, nearly walk on their hands in conjunction with their feet, and some of their body parts are not properly portioned. They even resemble animals by the way they act. This is of no concern to either Lucifer or Azrael because they have no idea what it supposed to look like. All they know is that Lucifer has accomplished what only the father should be capable of doing. "Witness the lies that have been afflicted upon us. The father is not almighty, and this is why. Now do you believe what I have told and showed you," Lucifer asks in a reassuring voice.

Azrael responds, "What choice do I have? The father is considered to be the only creator, but that is now a lie. Right now I'm not so sure that Alpha is the father of our kind because even the seed can recreate. If what I see is true, then why have we been deceived, Lucifer? And how can we be so sure that the father is or isn't the originator because I can honestly say that you may be the father," Azrael replies dubiously. Lucifer proceeds to fraudulently explain everything from why Alpha lied, to why there are different genders of the seed. He even explains his plan of conquering the father to prevent all creations from becoming slaves to the throne. "And if I can substantiate these facts to a few of the others, then everyone in the end will be free. All you have to do is walk with me on this Azrael, and you will have taken the first step towards autonomy. You have a special gift unlike many of the others, including myself. Discover it now; don't wait until you're called upon to know it. Then use it to your advantage. It's that simple. Do you understand," Lucifer asks?

Azrael finds truth in what Lucifer speaks and feels manipulated by the father. He observes Lucifer in this new light and wants the same freedom that was spoken of. At this point his spirit is filled with disappointment and anger towards the father for deceiving him, so he gravely looks Lucifer in the eyes and responds, "I do understand, and I want to help make things right. I praise you for helping me see things more clearly, and I'm in your debt. How may I return the favor," Azrael asks? Lucifer looks upon his creations running wild with no indications of discipline, and commands to Azrael, "Extend your hand and discover your gift, brother." With no hesitation, Azrael reaches out elegantly towards Eden and reveals his true power.

As previously observed, his aura is exposed to darkness as well. Lucifer is astonished by the power that Azrael possesses because it's nothing like what he presumed it to be. It's undoubtedly better than what he assumed on the grounds that this may be what subdues the Father. "Yes Azrael. I will give you the name of Death eclipse of all light, and you shall forever be the God of Mortality. Master your abilities to the fullest. You may be the deciding factor in my plan," Lucifer provokes while Azrael concentrates on perfection. Life was all that Eden knew, until it was touched by the hand of mortality.

The millions of species that existed ran wild with no care for each other when Lucifer first created them, now they are wild and killers thanks to Azrael. He gives them the instincts of survival based on his recent lesson from Lucifer about the father. Now the animals have a hunger. To satisfy that hunger, they have to eat, and to eat means they have to kill to subsist. Even the new seeds have to take life to endure in the name of Azrael, and each life that is loss, regardless of species, is absorbed by him like an essence to a soul collector. The only good thing that came from his power is that life only took what was needed to survive. In a diminutive degree of time Azrael masters his abilities. He seems more determined than Lucifer himself. However, Lucifer is powered by something more than just anger, and revenge.

He's driven by supremacy and gluttony as well. Conscripting additional allies is only the beginning to satisfying his greed, and he needs more followers as soon as possible while the Father is still at rest. "Azrael, what you have discovered, I now need for you to surpass. Instead of just Eden, master the secrets of all creations while I venture on a separate mission," Lucifer orders as he ventures off. Azrael responds, "Yes Lucifer, but what mission do you speak of now?" Lucifer turns rashly and replies, "We need more like us for the crusade. Alpha is not going to renounce the throne easily, so the more on our side, the quicker we obtain the throne," he stresses as he slowly fades from Azrael's presence.

As commanded, Azrael takes the time to enhance his abilities far beyond Eden. He begins to try to master the realm of the spirits and the cosmos. Meanwhile, Lucifer initiates his ultimate effort to gather enough partisans to form a new army, and for some reason it seems easier than what he expects. Something unique has happened to him besides the change of his appearance. Like Azrael, his gift is altered too. He is now the master of deception, and as a result every weak spirit is susceptible to his power. As Lucifer approaches behind Michael, his nearest target, he notices the energy in Spirit and decides to abandon his choice, considering the time it would take to convince such strength.

As he approaches his second target, he notices a difference in Spirit. This is the spirit of Sethrael, and it is slightly distorted and frail. "My thoughts are true then. I'm able to distinguish between weak and strong spirits. This is most beneficial, and with perfect timing. I shall now be known as the God of Deception," Lucifer boasts as he nears behind Sethrael. "One love, Sethrael. May I speak with you," Lucifer asks kindly? "You may," replies Sethrael while noticing Lucifer's appearance. "What is this essence that cloaks you? Is everything all right," Sethrael questions awkwardly. Lucifer smiles knowing that his choice of spirit is not much of a challenge for his craftiness, and speaks, "Everything is all right, Sethrael. I just want to answer those questions running through your spirit. Courtesy of the Father." Lucifer wraps his right arm around Sethrael's shoulder and guides him away from Michael's potential vision.

They both journey to the location near Azrael, which is where he proceeds to use virtually the same tactics on Sethrael. To his advantage, it works again. Sethrael vows to become Lucifer's counterpart for eternity for setting him free. "I'm indebted to you for eternity, Lucifer. How can I begin my repayment," Sethrael asks? Lucifer turns in Azrael's direction and speaks, "Witness the power that you too may have, Sethrael. In the likeness of Azrael, I only ask that you reach out your hand and discover your gift," Lucifer replies with a malevolent smile on his face. With no hesitation, Sethrael reaches out towards Eden to unravel his gift which instantly turns his aura dark as well. Simultaneously, Lucifer again feels as if he's growing stronger and more aware of things. Immediately, all of his creations become conscious of their surrounding environments and without delay develop into foolish, untamed, and violent beings. Instead of killing to survive, they are now wreaking havoc on any and every possible creature without the need to.

To Lucifer's surprise, Sethrael's power was amazing and unbelievable too. He has the power to make the creatures on Eden fight and destroy themselves by reigning chaos upon their heads while Azrael absorbs their lifeless essences. Lucifer smiles wickedly because he visualizes his plan coming together better and quicker than what he expects. He briefly turns to Sethrael and speaks, "You shall be granted the name of Seth, the God of Chaos. Master your abilities and extend them beyond Eden. Meanwhile, I shall depart one last time to encourage more like us," Lucifer says as he vanishes in the distance.

Lucifer knows that there isn't much time left, and that he can't continue to deceive one spirit at a time. He is also overconfident that he has mastered his own abilities because every time he fools a spirit, he notices that he gains power from it. First it was being able to detect weak from strong spirits, but now he feels as though he gained the power to hide his true appearance. By believing this, he makes an abrupt decision to recruit as many weak spirits as he can now, and then take them all back to show them his so-called truth.

"This is where I pull out all the odds, and complete my plan. Since I am the leader of the Army of God, then I should be able to make believers out of at least half of them," Lucifer says deviously. He then commences to put his theory to the test. The theory of disguising his true appearance. As expected, he can mask his aura, and this makes him overjoyed. "I now have the power to conceal my true manifestation. With this new power, I will have no difficulty achieving my goal," Lucifer speaks as he sets off to complete his objective. When he reaches the location of the Army of God, he immediately begins to single out the weak from the strong spirits.

Next, he selects a very small amount of the stronger ones too. Finally, he intentionally chooses the strongest spirit in the ranks of the army for reasons that are yet to be revealed. By the time he's done, thousands are gathered. This is well over half of the overall army. "To all the others that were not selected, please wander in spirit in order to honor the privacy of those that were. All else should walk with me," Lucifer speaks out to everyone. As usual, he comes prepared with a plan to persuade the selected. Even though he is the leader, he still needs orders to command them, and this is something they all know. Because of this, he decides to deviate from his plan, this time only, by telling the truth. As they all near a comfortable destination point, Lucifer begins to speak.

"One love to all my fellow comrades. The father has given me the power to provide the answers to all of your questions. I only ask that you allow me the chance to answer them all," he truthfully addresses the group. He then quickly glances to the left and notices that Aries, the most powerful spirit in which he has chosen, seems to have the most doubtful look on his face. This is probably because he feels that his questions can only be answered by the father. Lucifer counts on this happening and starts thinking,

"Instead of influencing each spirit separately, win over the strongest one and the rest will certainly follow." So he then points to Aries and says, "What about you, Aries? Ask now, and I shall answer all."

The crowd moves as Aries directs his way towards the front to respond. "One love, Lucifer," Aries politely addresses him face to face. In return, Lucifer respectfully nods his head as Aries continues. "For now, I only have two questions. Have we been summoned to perform our duties, and if not then why have we been selected out of all the others to gather here," he ends? These two questions are not what Lucifer expects, but they are answerable. To him it's like a challenge, and no challenge is too great to attempt. However, this test requires a moment of silence for the perfect deception.

In this moment of silence from Lucifer, Aries becomes eager for a response, but instead speaks remorsefully, "If I have offended you in any way by asking these questions, I'm sorry. That is not what I intended to do. Please forgive me, and make it so that the others may have their turns to ask." Lucifer smiles at Aries, but not for the reason he thinks. You see, Aries has just provided Lucifer with the answer to his own questions, and Lucifer ends his moment of silence to use it against him.

He replies, "In no way have you offended me, Aries. I was only receiving the answers to your questions through the Holy Spirit. The power that was bestowed upon me allows me to do that. In spite of this, your questions also triggered an adverse effect on me. Normally, I will only hear a response, but in this case I was given sight as well. Your questions are not ordinary," he interrupts his speech by unexpectedly falling to his knees and pretending to hold his head in agony. He portrays the pain as if he's being overpowered by the sight, "Aaahh. Too...much...power. Will...All...mighty...imperfect," Lucifer continues to cry out horrendously.

Aries is shocked at what's taking place right now because he feels as though it's his fault. Not knowing exactly what to do, he kneels down next to Lucifer, wraps his right arm around him, and looks towards the others and says, "My brothers, we all need to rethink our questions before we ask. Look at the pain that I alone have caused. I've obviously asked a question that should not have been asked. For that I should be the one to suffer this pain, not you, Lucifer," Aries cries out and continues. "I have withdrawn my questions and disregarded all thoughts associated with them, and the rest of you will do the same if your questions relate to mine. Are you all right, brother," Aries asks as a result of Lucifer breathing heavily? Lucifer's act slowly comes to an end while Aries increases his expression of concern. He wants to say yes to Aries right away, but something strange actually did occur during his fictitious performance.

He became aware of one crucial verity from the duration of being held by Aries. He was actually able to see the thoughts and feel the emotions of Aries. This simple fact gives him more ideas about how to use the new abilities that he's acquired throughout his quest. "Is it possible that I can now see the thoughts of others when touched? If so, then I wonder if it's likely to be reversed. Maybe I can permeate images of what I want them to see and with any luck brand them as my spawns," he continues to think quickly. At this point Aries grows more concerned and asks again, "Lucifer, are you all right?" Lucifer begins to mumble what he had stuttered earlier in a more serene voice while the others talk amongst themselves, "Too much power. Lies, deceit. The Will and Alpha; everything is imperfect. I don't think it was meant for you to ask those questions, or for me to see what I've seen, Aries," he replies wearily.

All at once there was an instant silence throughout the group. Aries removes his arm from Lucifer's shoulder, backs away, and responds, "What do you mean, brother? Everything created is perfect according to Alpha. This is blasphemy you speak of," he ends in an offended manner. Lucifer shakes off the fabricated pain and slowly stands to his feet facing Aries. The look on his face proclaims that he has also been lied to. Obviously, this is only a deceptive tactic for the purpose of misleading Aries, and Lucifer knows that this approach will leave him confused. This in turn will allow him to get within touching distance of Aries to reveal his own veracity; if his newly modified plan works.

Lucifer speaks in a tranquil manner, "How is it blasphemy when the answers are provided by the power of the Almighty? I have no clue of what the answers will be until the questions are asked. You asked me two questions that not only demanded an answer, but also required sight for my understanding. This opened new doors to my spirit that I was unprepared for. Basically I have only spoken what I've seen, but only you will understand the answer. Without a doubt, you are the beholder of the questions. So to help you understand, please allow me to show you, and maybe you can help me understand what I have seen, brother," Lucifer cleverly replies to Aries previous response. Aries is a little unsure about what he's hearing.

However, it all makes sense because he did ask demanding questions, and regardless of what he said previously, in spirit, he still wanted to know the answers. Lucifer knows this fact as well since he's more powerful than Aries. Yet and still, without provoking him, Lucifer gradually reaches out towards him and speaks again. "Please Aries, allow me to show you. Take my hand and all shall be seen in the eyes of the beholder." Still uncertain about the whole situation, Aries stares into Lucifer's eyes for a moment seeking to discern the circumstances single-handedly. Eventually, he cautiously reaches out in hopes to discover the answers because he can't fathom the idea that Lucifer may possibly be lying. Besides, such a thing in Himil is unheard of, and is an adequate reason to continue extending his hand.

As he gets closer to gripping Lucifer's hand he says, "I will allow you to show me what you've seen, Lucifer. However, if I see nothing, then I have no choice but to declare irreverence, and that is not my intention. I only aim to obtain the answers," Aries continues as he finally grasps Lucifer's right hand with his. Concurrently, Lucifer knows that this is a make or break situation according to that last response from Aries. He realizes that if he can't infuse images into Aries right now, then his plan will be ruined. While holding each other's right hands, Lucifer extends his left hand towards Aries' head. He says calmly as Aries leans forward in acceptance, "Kneel, brother, so that you won't be overwhelmed by the almighty power."

As Aries places his right knee on the ground while still holding Lucifer's right hand, Lucifer concentrates on projecting his ultimate plan. Aries bows his head and allows a few seconds to pass, but nothing occurs. However, he holds on to his beliefs that this will work, and doesn't declare irreverence. On the other hand, Lucifer begins to doubt himself, "I was certain that I would be capable of instilling my plan into his spirit, but nothing's happening. Why," he questions himself and then continues to think with poise? "It doesn't matter. I won't give up."

At the same time, everyone else becomes unsure about what is taking place and starts to look at each other. Whispers begin traveling throughout the crowd resulting in Lucifer feeling as though his plan may fail even more, but the sheer power of fortitude and the lust for absolute power triggers an extraordinary reaction. A bizarre power increasingly surges through his spirit generating what seems to be static electricity on the outside. He instantly knows that this is the ability he's seeking, and for his sake, quickly obtains control over it. The sheer sight of this unprecedented force immediately subdues the crowd, which allows Lucifer to regain confidence in his strategy. He also embraces a new idea of improvement to his plan and quickly conceives another to complement it.

This is the defining moment for him, and from this point on there's no turning back. "Since they are able to witness this new power that I possess, I will therefore portray it as the Almighty communicating through me. They will have no choice after that but to believe it," he contemplates while the energy brilliantly radiates through his eyes. By observing this wonder and not knowing exactly what's happening, everyone kneels in tandem and bow their heads as a sign of respect to the father. Aries maintains his composure without the slightest movement because he's determined to ascertain a resolution. Lucifer, in spite of this, slowly removes his left hand from Aries and speaks profoundly, "Straighten your head and address your father, Aries," he inappropriately speaks as the Almighty. Aries unquestionably raises his head believing that father is in Lucifer, and everyone else does the same. Lucifer smiles because he envisions the wait to be over, but superficially his smile is believed to be an approval of their greetings.

As before, his power quickly increases twofold as a result of the thousands that are falling victim to his ruse. It now begins to emerge from his eyes slowly following a path to his left hand. As the power nears his wrist, he gradually raises his arm and gently places his hand on Aries' forehead. Aries shows no sign of trepidation and remains motionless. Again, Lucifer begins to imitate the father as the energy envelops his hand, "You will now reap the knowledge to the answers you seek, Aries. Behold," he declares in a divine voice! Instantly his spirit becomes tainted with the thoughts of Lucifer's visions. He foresees why all questions can't be answered at the same time, false plans of Alpha enslaving all angels for the love of the key, and life being created from the hands of others.

Lucifer is enjoying every moment of this because he feels the faith in the spirit of Aries dissipating with every second that passes. At this particular moment he's sure that he has his army. However, he doesn't want to get too overconfident, and so he ends the trickery by collapsing to his knees as if the father had quickly departed his spirit. Eventually his hand slips away from Aries and the power surges slowly vanish.

While Aries breathes intensely and Lucifer fakes it, he is also timid about what he has seen. "Father, why show me that your plan is imperfect when perfection is consummate," he inquires under the impression that Alpha is still within Lucifer. Lucifer, on the other hand, calms his breathing and stands to his feet. He then offers his right hand to Aries as an aid for standing and replies, "Rise, my brother, for the father has answered your questions." Aries grabs his hand and stands up looking befuddled because Lucifer's facial expression is as if nothing has transpired. He turns around to see if the group has the same expression, but again is even more confused because they all have an astonished look on their faces.

By observing the situation, he comes to a conclusion as he turns back towards Lucifer, "Brother, you have partially witnessed the answer to my deepest thoughts beforehand, and this time the father has spoken through you to fulfill my uncertainties. My comrades have also witnessed this unusual power from the Almighty, and are amazed. Did they not see what transpired? Honestly, that's the least of my concerns. Why do I feel insecure? Only I can answer that. However, my issue is that what I have seen creates a serious problem with the father being almighty," he turns and loudly announces this to the others. Lucifer maintains the same facial expression in order to camouflage his true masquerade, but on the inside he smiles. In contrast, whispers ignite throughout the crowd at variance.

Aries raises his arms in response to the chattering and continues in a peaceful tone, "Stay calm, my brothers. What I am about to speak will not be blasphemy. The questions that I asked before left the slightest room for pondering more. Please, allow me to explain. The first question answered more than what I expected because it was destined for the ultimate answer. This includes the answer to the second question also. You see, I queried the Almighty's strength and abilities through Lucifer. From that I learned the deepest and most eccentric wonders of the father's spirit. If the father is truly the Almighty, then why is the power of creation not limited to Alpha," he questions evocatively while whispers quickly rekindle? He starts to get annoyed because he believes that they should understand, and so turns to Lucifer for aid in helping them. "Lucifer, I feel that you and I have the same understanding. Please explain to them what we've seen together."

Lucifer looks Aries directly in the eyes and says, "I'm sorry brother. I really have no recollection of what you experienced just now. I only remember bits and pieces from the first time you asked your questions because I had the power to personally answer it," he says with a straight face. In a sense, Aries understands that maybe the answers are meant for his eyes only. He rubs his chin with his right hand as he looks down and thinks out loud, "What if it isn't," he points in Lucifer's direction and continues. "Is it possible that you may be able to show everyone what I spoke of like you did for me, Lucifer? But hear me out first," he puts both of his hands up and continues. "The power that surged through my spirit was tremendous. It even put you on your knees the first time, Lucifer. I believe that if we all join hands, the force will still be strong enough to create a torrent of energy though every single one of us. This may allow them to behold what I've seen," he says desperately.

Lucifer doubtfully gazes upon the thousands, slowly shakes his head from side to side, and then looks back at Aries and replies,

“That could actually work, except there’s one problem. Your questions have already been answered making it unnecessary to fulfill twice for the same spirit. Hhmm! Maybe if someone else asked a similar question,” Lucifer cleverly pauses. “The time has finally come to claim my army,” he thinks as Aries unknowingly interrupts his thoughts. “I have faith that it’ll work, brother. Although, who should ask it,” he inquires? Lucifer looks around at everyone and replies, “I will ask the question in spirit because of my connection with the father’s power. It’s only right that I do so. But before I do, I need everyone to hold hands with Aries and myself to make this work,” he kindly requests. At this time he doesn’t know if he has enough power to make all of them see, but he does believe that he can reach at least half of them with his visions.

After a few moments pass, everyone joins hands. Lucifer glances at them all and then speaks directly to Aries, “I won’t make you a promise, but I will try my best to reach them all. Have faith, brother,” he says with a smile while turning towards everyone else. “I need you all to think about these questions deep down and try to connect with each other spiritually. I will do the same,” he concludes by bowing his head and closing his eyes. Everybody does the same and then patiently waits. A few seconds pass and his eyes begin to charge again, but this time a lot stronger than before. His power had increased tenfold because of the trust he gained from all of them put together. He uses this extra boost of power to focus all of his strength into energy, and it becomes so intense that every angel feels its presence before being touched. Even his spirit begins to radiate with waves of energy.

Without wasting anymore time, he releases his incredible show of power amongst the group, and, as hoped, it eventually spreads throughout the thousands. He douses them all with his impious ideas and visions, including all of the tactics in which he used to mislead Azrael and Sethrael. He even performs his most deluded tactic yet. He implants a vision in which the Almighty's power can be challenged and surpassed by any spirit deemed worthy. And of course, he makes it all seem acceptable courtesy of the father. A short time passes and the propaganda ultimately comes to an end. He introduces every dishonest notion and theory possible. No stone is left unturned, excluding the conception of war. He has special reason for this one.

Aries opens his eyes along with everyone else, and slowly turns towards Lucifer. "So it's you. You're the special one that proved the Almighty's power to be limited. Why didn't you speak of this earlier," he asks ominously? Lucifer innocently replies as he turns and walks away, "Follow me." Not knowing exactly what to do, Aries follows him along with all the others. At the moment this all happens, I complete my rest back in Himil and I address Gabriel. "As my herald, come and convey this message to every spirit." Gabriel reverently kneels near the throne to be touched by my hand. I embrace him and speak, "I have completed my rest, and I call upon all things in existence to carry out their duties. Also, notify Lucifer and Michael that their special attributes are now essential. Go and touch every spirit with the word. It is time," I order while Gabriel's spirit illuminates with the message. He then replies as he turns to leave, "Thy Will be done, father." Since he's Alpha's courier, he's able to detect the spiritual trajectory of all life, making no message undeliverable. As he passes these life forces and spirits, he touches them and instantly transmits the message, including Michael. However, as he passes by the Almighty's army he notices that there are a few thousand absent. It's not his mission to worry about why, so therefore he continues his journey.

Meanwhile, Lucifer leads the group towards Eden while answering Aries' previous question, "It's true that the father gave me the power to answer all. In that perspective, I was fraught with the absolute truth. If I would've told you in advance...," he was politely interrupted by Aries. "Then there's no way that we would've believed you." Lucifer continues as they get closer to the location of Eden, "That's right. Only the father openly speaks, until now," he pauses as Eden becomes visible. He stretches out his hands towards it and continues, "Because now all of you know the truth. You were deemed worthy of it."

There is an immediate silence and halt of movement throughout the multitude. Azrael and Sethrael are off in the distance putting the final touches on mastering their abilities, but it's difficult for the group to see what's actually going on from their standpoints. Aries finally breaks silence and asks, "This is your creation, brother?" Lucifer resumes walking and replies as Gabriel appears in the distance behind them, "Yes, and it's more to it than what you see now. Listen everyone, I have given you the choice to know what you know now, and I have shown you what truths really exist. I hide nothing from my brothers. But the father, ohh the father, tried to hide what was known from us all until it was too late," he announces. At this point Gabriel stops advancing forward in disarray, and decides to listen instead.

"Blasphemy, it's all blasphemy," an unknown member yells. Lucifer continues provokingly, "It's not blasphemy, brother. Think about it. If the father is almighty, then why is rest required? Also, why can't we use our gifts now instead of waiting for them to be called upon? I'll tell you why. If we knew then what we know now, then the father would have no control. Rest was vital because Alpha needed to recover…hint, hint…more imperfections. The lie is this. Power is granted to all when the Almighty calls upon it," he speaks convincingly. Gabriel can't believe what he's hearing, so he quickly departs unnoticed to warn the father because he knows that this could lead to war. Lucifer continues to preach, "Power is not granted by the father. That was only spoken to keep you enslaved to the Almighty's Will. You already possess the power, and you can use it at will. If you don't believe what I'm saying, then I would be wrong if you extended your hand to discover it and nothing happens. Am I right," he instigates the group. He knows that if they raise their hands and reveal their gifts, then he has them?

One unknown member extends his hand and speaks to everyone, "There's only one way to know the truth. If we raise our hands and nothing happens, then the Almighty will hear of this, but if something does, then enough said. Lucifer is right." Aries neither agrees nor disagrees, but he does have concerns about who is right or wrong. So he stands his ground to watch. Whatever the case may be, he honestly believes Lucifer to be right from what he's seen so far. Anyhow, everyone finally agrees to the no lose situation and raises their hands.

Aries was the only one not to raise his hand even though he believed Lucifer. Seconds pass and nothing happens. Lucifer is expecting this because he knows that he doesn't have their overall trust. To him all they need is a little motivation. He knows that Aries is on his side by observing his spiritual essence, and he decides to use him one last time. "It won't work without your beliefs, Aries, since it takes trust to purify doubt." Aries turns towards the group and speaks, "Lucifer is right. We all have doubt because of the answers that the father has provided us. Out of reverence I shall raise my hand with absolute faith in hopes that you all do the same. I want to finally know the whole truth. What about you," he concludes as he raises his left hand?

After Aries makes his speech, everyone agrees with him and converts their doubt into faith. Things immediately start to happen. First, each of their essences begins to grow darker as previously displayed by Lucifer, Azrael, and Sethrael. Additionally, everyone's spiritual characteristics begin to change. Instead of having the armor of light as protection now, they are all enveloped in dark armor, and it's seemingly stronger. Finally, they each gain knowledge of war and the power of the sinister sword. Their minds are now completely corrupt by Lucifer's mendacity, and he loves it. Since Aries is the strongest of them all, he gains much more power than he imagines and everyone knows this as well as Lucifer. He's instantly considered the decision maker and general of the group.

With power rushing through his hands, Aries turns to Lucifer and says, "We all owe you an apology, brother. From what we have discovered here, the father is the one who hid the truth from our eyes, but you shined light on these lies and deceit. I command us all to kneel in tribute to Lucifer," he orders and kneels first while the rest follow. This act alone triggers a much more intense power surge through Lucifer's spirit, causes his aura to reveal itself, and increases in size spiritually. Lucifer, now the largest angel, says to Aries, "You shall be known as the God of War, Aries, from now until eternity. Use your gift proudly, and the rest will follow your lead," he speaks as the darkness in his spirit is at its peak and greed is quickly becoming...

Chapter 4: The Downside of War.

"Father, I must report that I've failed to convey your message in its entirety," Gabriel quickly testifies. I slowly lean forward and reply, "Failure is the equivalent to a broken spirit therefore does not exist. The spirit cannot be broken." Gabriel understands, kneels, and then replies, "Forgive me, father. I didn't deliver your message to Lucifer, Azrael, Sethrael, and what seemed to be over half of your army. When I came upon them, I noticed some sort of unusual gathering. At that point I overheard Lucifer speaking to the entire group, apart from Azrael and Sethrael. They were further away illicitly utilizing their gifts while being surrounded by a peculiar essence. Excluding them, Lucifer spoke untruths on the Almighty name to your army. I left only to notify you of this, my Lord," he timidly ends his report.

I gradually lean back on the throne and gently speak these words, "Everything that happens, is. Everything that does not occur is one in the same. Listen Gabriel, I have embedded in all life the luxury of judgment. If you think it's best to walk by my side, then Lucifer may think to believe otherwise. Because of what he believes, there will be a war, and this will bring about an imbalance within the heavens. This disparity and the end of day by my hand will be written in the stars. Knowing that I am Alpha, I will end it as the Omega," I announce peacefully.

Gabriel stands proudly and responds, "I will deliver this message to each and all creations, and I will have no fear because failure does not exist in your graciousness, father," he ends while turning to leave my presence. I reply encouragingly, "For your courage and devotion, you shall not be harmed. Also, deliver a new message to Michael. He will become the leader of the army. Call upon each and everyone not tainted by Lucifer's misconceptions and prepare for the expected," I conclude. Gabriel acknowledges the requests and exits. His faith is strong, and because of that, I surround him with a barrier. He is to be untouched as a messenger for as long as he exists as such.

While Gabriel continues to convey the message to Michael and all the other nearby creations, Lucifer finally reunites with Azrael and Sethrael. “My brothers, it is time. The lies and deceit that were forced upon us will now be removed from our heads. Use your gifts that have been mastered for the greater good and we shall reign supreme,” Lucifer addresses the group and continues. “Take a look at what we have to gain, Aries. This is Eden, the perfect creation. This will be everyone’s new playground for as long as it exists by my hand. Embrace it, for it will then acknowledge every single one of you as gods,” he says as he turns and points towards Eden. He knows that desire will in turn fuel their ambitions to win the war. At the same time Lucifer ends his speech, Gabriel enters his presence to deliver the Almighty’s message.

Gabriel speaks without fear as he stands two feet from Lucifer, “Lucifer and all, the father has sent me with a message to everyone. First, I will reiterate a previous undelivered message,” he says. “Alpha has rested. The time for all creations to prepare for the key is here. This is the message that I should’ve delivered to you all before, but I overheard your blasphemy, Lucifer, and I fled to warn the father,” Gabriel says as he’s rudely interrupted by Aries. “Blasphemy? Huh! You have no idea what you speak of. Your strength of faith belongs to an imposter. How can your father be almighty when Lucifer has the same power to create? Witness Eden, and then be silent on what you’re ignorant of,” Aries points angrily towards Eden. Lucifer also interrupts, “Your father no longer has power over us. So what you speak of is pointless. We will open the eyes of all creations to the truth, and you will thereafter follow,” Lucifer says as Gabriel continues. “You speak too soon, Lucifer. The father knew of this war, and so, sent me with this message instead. Knowing that I am Alpha, I will end it as the Omega," he speaks as the Almighty. He then walks up and stands directly in front of Lucifer's face and says, "In other words, what you speak of is pointless, and you have no chance of winning. And these are my words," he replies with authority.

Azrael quickly moves in on Gabriel with the power of death and says, "How dare you! Let me finish him, Lucifer?" Lucifer reaches out his left arm and blocks Azrael from continuing and replies, "No. That won't be necessary. He will retract his testimony in due time, but then it'll be too late," he concludes as he removes his arm. Gabriel stares at Azrael and speaks, "It's never too late to change your faith. You've already done it once. This goes for all of you as well," he replies while pointing at everyone, and then quickly exits to continue his mission. "He will go back and report everything. Then they'll know how many of us there are, and probably how to counter us. Why didn't you let me finish him, Lucifer," Azrael questions?

Lucifer turns to him with a smirk on his face and replies, "Because we need him just as much as his father. He's already accepted his gift as a messenger, and obviously doesn't want to change it. Furthermore, nobody else will be able to outdo him at it. This makes it easier for us to send the word of our victory through him, or else he suffers. Unless you want to take his position at becoming a courier, I suggest you let him do his job," he deviously replies.

In the middle of Azrael and Lucifer's discussion, Aries uses his remarkable gift to power up the army's swords and spiritual armor. He even strengthens their knowledge of how to fight strategically by embedding in their spirits the art of war. All of the commotion instantly grabs the attention of Lucifer, Azrael, and Sethrael. They are all amazed as Aries completes this unexpected but startling marvel. He faces Lucifer and eagerly asks with a smile, "When do we fight?" Lucifer slowly raises his arms, spreads them out and replies to everyone commandingly, "We fight now."

Aries turns towards the group and says, “Go, my brothers. Journey to Himil, take the throne, capture the impure one, and detain anyone who stands in your path.” Lucifer lowers his arms and the group immediately departs.

Meanwhile, Michael approaches the throne, kneels, and speaks, “Father, I have received your calling. How did things elevate so quickly to this, and how will I begin to undertake this difficult assignment,” he says. I reply to him, “Faith is the cause and the answer, Michael. What you believe in has the power to overcome, but be careful so that you won’t abuse it. If so, you will then end up like Lucifer. He is weak with envy, and strong with deceit. Nevertheless, you are now much stronger than he is in spirit. Keep this faith and you will triumph,” I reply as Michael, without a hassle, accepts it and stands. He courageously turns his back to me and speaks, “I know what I must do, father. And it will be done.” He takes two steps forward to exit and notices that his spirit energy has strengthened and quickly replicates a small sword in his right hand. Without the slightest hesitation, he knows what it is for and continues to exit.

I speak to him as he leaves, “Michael, the Sword of Piety has the power to vanquish the evil within the spirit of all creations. Your faith is the source of its power, and will determine the result of valor that it occupies. While your devotion remains strong the power of the sword is boundless, and vice versa. Use it wisely,” I conclude. At the same time that Michael gathers what is left of the army, Lucifer and his crusade have nearly completed their journey back to Himil. They are so close that the obscurity of their essences combined, can be seen in the distance. Michael isn’t afraid because his faith is so strong, but he knows some of the others are. He finishes gathering up everyone, quickly explains the situation, and reveals his sword to all of them. “I know that some of you don’t know exactly what’s happening right now, and I also know that some of you fear the unknown. I too feared the indefinite, and so I asked the father how to accomplish it. Faith, my brothers. Faith is the key. Alpha bestowed upon me this sword as a sign of gratitude for my strength in spirit," he says as he raises his hand to present it. "Each of you has the same power within, and as long as you believe in it, the sword will conquer all that's evil," he says.

Uriel decides to speak, "I believe strongly in what the father can do, but look at how many of us there are, Michael. It's just not enough to take on Lucifer and his army. He's taken well over half of the original army. Besides, most of were not blessed with the gift to fight. And look at how small your sword is. That thing will only upset Lucifer even more," he ends his statement timidly as the others begin to mumble. Michael turns his back towards the group and says to Uriel, "And you were chosen to be the angel of salvation, Uriel? Huh, looks to me like you will become the captive, along with the rest of you," he scornfully replies. Immediately the size of his sword increases on account of his faith, and he begins to fearlessly sprint towards Lucifer's army unaccompanied by the others.

Lucifer recognizes Michael's spirit approaching and says, "Fool. Does he really believe that he can defeat us all by himself," he laughs hysterically? Aries replies, Impossible. We are too mighty as a whole. Not even...," Aries stops in the middle of his sentence and eventually stops running because Michael just took a leap so tremendous from a distance that seems impossible to his eyes. Lucifer immediately speaks, "Everyone, halt." Right away, everyone ceases movement and waits for new orders. Lucifer continues while directing his comments to Aries, "He will eventually land. When he does, he'll be vulnerable for a short period. Try to measure his trajectory so that we'll be near him when he touches down, and then take him out," he orders Aries.

Aries gives the order to the army, and they wait anxiously for him to land. Everyone's heads are straight up with their eyes on

Michael waiting for the opportunity to strike as he draws closer to them. They are so fixed on him that they don't realize what's emerging in the distance. Uriel and the others have gained their own strength and faith to fight for morality and righteousness. The Sword of Piety is acquired by every one of them, and they embrace it proudly ready for war. As Michael draws nearer, Aries gives an order, "Ready your swords and shields, and position yourselves for battle. Remember, as soon as he touches down, don't hesitate to strike," he commands knowing that Michael's only a few seconds from impact. However, Michael's faith becomes so strong that it illuminates his spirit and enhances his sword again to an astonishing fiery blue magnitude. The sword is now about the length of his height, which is about six and a half angel feet; twice the size of the largest homan.

Nevertheless, with both hands, he lifts the sword over his head with flames discharging like lightning, and screams furiously, "The Hand of God." His voice echoes as he drives the sword in the ground forcefully as he lands. At the same time that this occurs, Aries screams, "Now." However, the energy released from the impact of the blade is literally a blue firestorm shock wave that instantly immobilizes hundreds. It even affects the others by pushing them back a few feet. Lucifer and Aries are not impressed at all though because they were born of strong spirits as well. On the other hand, Michael is too focused to care. In his spirit, he is here to fight for the father.

Therefore, immediately after the firestorm ends, he extracts his sword from the ground, sprints towards the others, and begins to fight solo. He doesn't know that the others are on their way. So one by one Lucifer's soldiers are toppled by Michael's exceptional fighting techniques and hundreds more single-handedly fall before Lucifer decides to end the nonsense. Lucifer begins to move through the crowd as Michael continues to fight and says, "Amazing kicks and punches, Michael. And a nice sword too, but you shouldn't have come alone, because you can't defeat us all by yourself. Practically it's a guaranteed victory for us. Do you have so strong a faith that the father will assure your success against thousands," he taunts as he catches a glimpse of the Almighty Army appearing over the horizon? "Oh, I see. You didn't think that I would notice, huh? You were setting us up the whole time for an ambush. You wanted to catch us off guard so that your partners could take us down all at once," he snickers and continues. "Well, your comrades will perish along with you. This ends now," he says while pushing his way through the crowd towards Michael.

Michael quickly looks around in the midst of fighting curious of what Lucifer spoke of. "It's not a lie. The others are indeed nearby. They have found their faiths deep within," he thinks and smiles to himself. However, he continues to fight, and notices that Lucifer is slowly growing in size and changing form as he advances forward. "What is this? Do you really think that you can frighten my faith away, Lucifer? I'll show you fear," Michael says as he forces his enemies back without touching them by using a powerful push with his right hand. What seems to be the same moment, he kneels down on his right knee with the sword in his right hand, quickly swings it around to his left side between his thigh and waist, and holds it there with his left arm stretched out across his face. This all happens so fast that it literally looks instantaneous with numerous slow motion-like after images following the primary motion.

At least three hundred angels pile on top of Michael in hopes of containing him until Lucifer arrives to the front line. What they don't realize is that Michael has formed a barrier around his spirit with his left arm, and is charging his sword with his right hand. Lucifer is not sure of what he's up to or capable of, and so he decides to slow his progress. Michael continues charging this ultimate technique and at the same time praying for it to even the odds for his army. Lucifer figures out that it's a trap and promptly orders, “Let him free. It’s another trap.” Some of them actually have the chance to climb off and back away, but for most it’s too late. Without hesitation, Michael unleashes a powerful spin move of energy from kneeling position to standing position as he shouts, “Breath of Retribution.” Everyone that’s on him, including many more still within range, is blown more than a hundred feet back and knocked unconscious from the wave burst. The force is so powerful that it drains Michael’s as he continues spinning, and decommissions one third of Lucifer’s overall army at the same time.

As he concludes his technique, he draws a line on the ground with the sword from left to right in the course of his last spin while looking down. “Earning a victory will be much sweeter than a guaranteed one, Lucifer,” Michael says. Still looking down, he remains motionless and hides all signs of fatigue by mocking Lucifer’s previous statement. His faith allows him to recover fast, and Lucifer doesn’t see it because he’s becoming agitated. He looks up and notices that Uriel and the others have jumped from a distance, and gets upset with what has happened to his fellow colleagues, and says, “Seth and Aries, show these imbeciles the chaos of war. Azrael, go forth and bring death to all of them that fall to my power, and make the rest suffer while I handle this nuisance,” he says irritably while cracking his knuckles and increasing his size by at least three times greater than Michael’s. He sprouts wings, a tail divided at the end, split hooves for feet, and claws for hands. His spirit becomes pitch black, and his murky essence curves upward from his feet appearing to form horns as it nears the top of his head.

Michael maintains his posture and notices how enormous Lucifer has grown by observing his shadow, and without any expressions remains motionless to recover faster. Aries orders what’s left of the Army of Darkness to attack the Army of God, and Seth joins the fight by bringing chaos as ordered. The war has officially commenced with both armies. As Lucifer completes his growth and swiftly approaches, Michael finally looks up with a nauseating stare and says, "Is that it? You've desecrated your spirit for this? Really, all you've done is gone from being the most beautiful angel, to the ugliest and largest fraud, period," he taunts as Lucifer starts to run full speed at him grunting in anger. He holds his ground and continues to taunt, "It should be a name for such an appearance. I think I will call it fiendish, and devilish. Your name is no longer Lucifer." Lucifer, now extremely angry, begins to speak at the same time, "You will suffer for your ignorance, Michael." Michael continues, "Your new name will be Satan," and ends as Satan grunts and vigorously swings at him with his left hand.

Michael, still exhausted, decides to conserve his energy by only dodging to the right. He knows that his faith is allowing him to power up quickly, but he just isn't strong enough at this moment to seriously injure Satan. Upon missing his swing, Satan immediately swings with his right, and Michael evades to the left. Now irritated by Michael not attacking, he uses both of his hands as one fist, and charges it while raising it above his head. Michael squats down as Satan smashes it down forcefully, and back flips away from it as it collides. However, Satan planned on him doing just that, and sends a shock wave of continuous energy outwards after Michael flips out of harms way. He knows that it's a slim to none chance of Michael dodging this when he lands.

Michael, now energetic and ready to fight back, lands from the back flip and in the blink of an eye jumps back towards the direction of Satan escaping his shock wave by a mere inch from the tip of his toes. Michael grips the sword with his right hand, swiftly positions it behind him parallel to his waist, and continues, "I will defeat you at all costs." He clinches a fist with his left arm extended, and thrusts his sword into Satan's left knee. Then he quickly removes it, rotates while swinging to the right with his back facing Satan, and slashes his right knee. Michael performs this combo so fast that when Satan falls to his knees growling from the excruciating pain, he has already landed and begun to walk away with the sword relaxed on his right shoulder.

He comes to a halt with his back still towards Satan, and removes the sword from his shoulder. He sticks it in the ground, calmly rests the palm of his right hand on the handle, and says, "One way or another, you will remember how to bow in our father's name and repent. Renounce your hate now before it's too late, and perhaps you might be forgiven. Otherwise...," he says as Satan interrupts by laughing hysterically. He chuckles for a short period and then says, "Otherwise what? No, no, no. Don't tell me. Let me guess," he says while shaking his head and hands. "You will vanquish me in your father's name. Is that it," he snickers. Michael removes his hand from the handle, looks over his left shoulder and replies, "I asked you to repent once and you ignored my request. Now, I'm telling you to," he says in an infuriated voice.

Satan begins to recover quickly from Michael's sword wounds and replies sarcastically, "Huh. Let me tell you something. I have a special gift also. As a matter of fact I have a few, but this specific one allows me to become skilled at anything I desire in a small fraction of time. Basically, the whole time that you've been hopping around enchantingly with your sword using your fancy fighting methods...," he continues while reducing his size back to normal. "...I've recorded every principal, every sound, and every technique that you've irresponsibly demonstrated. I will defeat you with your own gift, and then I'll personally destroy your army with my bare hands," he grunts and stands up.

As Satan completes his healing process, the Army of God begins to gradually gain the advantage over the Army of Darkness with Uriel leading the way. He had seen from a distance how well Michael fought and it uplifted his spirit, as well as the others. From

Michael's standpoint, his feelings about their performance are identical. Their faiths, again, increases dramatically; however, regardless of how big the disadvantage is getting there is still no stopping the Army of Darkness from fighting either. At this point, he withdraws his sword from the ground and turns around facing Satan. "I could care less what your gift is, Satan. Your time will soon be up," he says as he begins gradually walking towards him to end this confrontation.

Satan fully extends his left arm upwards, and points with his right hand as Michael starts to speed up the pace. "You won't survive long enough to witness that time even if it does exist," he replies as streaks of lightning start to absorb in his left hand. He's manifesting his spiritual essence into a sword resembling the Sword of Piety. As the sword appears in the grips of his palm, Michael slightly hesitates in disbelief because there's no way that Satan can summon or wield the sword. What he doesn't know is that Satan can read how strong and weak a spirit is, and by Michael's sword decreasing in size, it only becomes more apparent.

Michael begins dashing towards him in hopes to stop him before the sword completely forms. He jumps at full speed, spins, and tries to roundhouse kick Satan in the face with his right foot. However, Satan ducks the attack only to find that a left foot is approaching the same side of his face in the midst of regaining his posture. He quickly blocks the kick with his right forearm, palms Michael's chest in mid air with the same hand, and power slams him on his backside while his left arm remains in position. Michael drops his sword and groans in pain while Satan laughs. "You can't stop me now, Michael. I too possess the ability to carry Piety, and I owe it all to you," he says as the sword completely materializes.

He finally lowers his left arm with the sword in his hand, leans over and grabs Michael by the neck with his right hand, and hoists him above his head. He grips the sword tighter in his left hand and says, “You’ve underestimated my power, Michael, and for that you will suffer. I would offer you the opportunity to join me, but your spirit is dedicated only to your father...,” he says as he draws the sword back and continues. “...who you will see no more.” He uses all of his might to drive the sword into Michael’s right side, yanks it out, and then does it over and over again. After a few times, Satan removes the sword and slams him again by the neck.

Michael’s blade gradually shrinks while he lies still, and Satan’s sword transforms into a pitch-black essence of fire. “Now for that army of yours,” he says as he picks up Michael’s sword and steps on his head while walking away. He gets about ten paces away from Michael and hears, “Your quarrel lingers with me you retched fiend.” Satan stops dead in his tracks and promptly turns around, but nothing is there. “Whaaat! What kind of trickery is this,” he replies with anger and confusion in his voice? Michael replies, “It is no trickery, Satan. It is only a simple truth. You told me the secret of your power which was a huge mistake. If I heard you right, you learn from observing, meaning that your control and power is limited. My power comes from faith, and will be forever limitless.”

Satan, fidgeting, looks around from left to right and says, “What you’re doing is not going to work, so stop trying to confuse me and stop wasting my time. You think that you’re smart by trying to recover again. Well, when I get my hands on you this time, I’m going to use both swords to rip you apart.” Michael replies, “I’m not the deceitful one. That’s your game. However, if you want clarification, I’ll keep it short and simple. Your sword is fictitious and weak, and combined with your spirit. My sword is almighty and pure, and I am one with it,” he says as his sword’s essence begins to wrap itself around and down Satan’s arm undetected.

Satan begins to get more agitated and says, “Come out and fight me, right now. Let’s end this,” not noticing that Michael’s essence of the blade has now completely encased his body. Michael replies, "It's over, and you've lost," he ends as he appears in front of Satan's face. Lucifer tries to swing but the sword puts an inescapable grip over his entire spirit causing him to fall backwards. He continuously tries to fight his way out of it, but it only gets worse. "No, no, no. How is this possible? I am more powerful than you. This can't be done to me," he continues to ramble on while Michael kneels beside him. He replies, "Obviously, your spirit resides somewhere else because you didn't hear a word I said. I'll say it one more time for the records. My sword and I are one. Basically I transferred my spirit into it before you had a chance to thrust yours into me. You actually cut an inert mimic of my spirit. The key was to get you to pick up my sword. I think I did a pretty good job of that," he says as he grabs hold of the visible portion of the handle.

He bows his head while holding it and says, "And you've underestimated one more detail as well. The true sword has the ability to suppress the evil within...," he closes his eyes and continues. "...and then you shall be judged. With that said, Michael begins silently praying. The sword starts to glow around Satan's body causing him to tremble involuntarily. "What is this? What's happening," Satan asks insufferably? Without a sound Michael continues to remain motionless. Satan begins to struggle violently trying to escape the trap, but the sword shines even brighter by matching his strength and then raising its own.

At last Michael opens his eyes and replies, "Your strength and powers have been decreased, and you have been silenced so that your malevolence will not spread any further. However, this is not permanent unless the Almighty decides otherwise at your tribunal," he rises and continues. "But indisputably, you will be chastised for your transgressions," he concludes as the sword continues to drain every bit of evil energy from Satan's spirit. He then grabs the handle of the sword again and it unwraps itself from around Satan's body. It redevelops in his right hand more powerful than before. The sword has, without a doubt, retained the strength of Satan and converted it into the power of virtue.

Michael looks down at Satan's weak and defenseless body and says, "With your power and mines combined, I shall put an end to this ridiculous war." He raises the sword above his head, and it slowly drifts from his hand into the heavens rapidly spinning as it rises. This time instead of glowing, it vanishes and instantly reappears directly above the two armies as they fight while becoming only visible to the eyes of righteousness. Aries and his group cannot see it. Michael bends down and hoists Satan over his shoulder to carry him back and says, "No need to worry about your army of minions, Satan. They will lose. And as for you, it's time for your judgment." Satan's eyes slowly close to Michael leaping over and pass the battle, in route back to Himil.

Aries catches sight of Michael leaping over them with Satan on his shoulder and cries out, "Azrael, Seth, stop him. Don't let him reach Himil." Azrael and Seth both acknowledge the order and jumps in the direction of Michael, but something unusual occurs. They both collapse incredibly hard. "What just happened, and why do I suddenly feel drained of strength," Azrael questions while breathing heavily? Seth, also wheezing, picks himself up and replies, "I don't know, but I feel the same way. Did we hit something," he asks with his hands out?

At this point Uriel and the others that are still conscious stops fighting and back flips out of danger, while Aries raises his hand to cease battle on behalf of the Army of Darkness. He thinks that the Army of God is retreating because of Michael's departure. Instead, the Army of God forms numerous ranks within a safe distance and duplicates Michael's last sword technique. Only their swords didn't quite disappear like his had. The essence remained within their hands. It was almost as if Michael somehow instructed them to do this, telepathically, as he passed overhead. Anyhow, completely confused with this unexpected situation, Aries quickly looks around and notices that Azrael and Seth are on the ground behind him, and yells, "I mean now, before he gets too far. We cannot allow him to reach Himil. In fact, I want everybody to target Michael since his coward army is no longer a threat," he yells out while pointing in the direction of Himil.

Before Aries finishes his command, the power from the swords of the Army of God expels a streamline of energy towards Michael's sword merging as one beam, and increases the strength of the barrier by a hundred fold. Again, only the eyes of the righteous can see the barrier along with Michael's sword. To Aries and the others, it looks as though the enemy is simply pointing upwards and releasing beams of light in their direction. Azrael and Seth arise from the surface looking around and still wondering what hit them. Azrael says to Seth, "I'm not going anywhere until I figure out what hit us." Seth replies, "Same here."

Meanwhile, about a few dozen angels immediately follow his orders and leaps towards Michael. Before they even reach two feet off the surface, power distributes from Michael's sword in each angle that they're jumping from. On contact, it spreads throughout their spirits like a huge surge of static electricity and quickly drains every ounce of their force. They fall unconscious while others take the leap unaware of what's taking place at the moment. Aries, on the other hand, is aware. He begins to briefly contemplate what's happening.

"It's another one of Michael's traps, and I fell for it. No more. This time I'll have to overcome it myself because Lucifer isn't here to help me," he scans the area looking for a way out while others continue to jump and fall. He starts in the direction of the Army of God and traces the beams back to what seems like a nowhere spot. Then he starts to notice that his comrades are being knocked unconscious by energy emitting from this same location, and thinks out loud as more continue to try, "That's it." Azrael and

Seth turn and respond simultaneously, “What’s it?” Aries continues, “Well, I sort of noticed that Michael was swordless as he passed overhead. I didn’t think anything of it because I was only focused on retrieving Lucifer. And that’s just it. He wanted us to think nothing of it so that we would all try to follow him and become blindsided by the power of his sword. But I’ve figured it out. Because there it is, right there...,” he points towards the location of the sword and then uses his finger to follow the path of a falling angel as he continues, “...bringing us down.”

Azrael and Seth look at each other even more confused with their hands out. Seth replies, “There what is, Aries? I don’t see anything but trails of light flowing towards the enemy.” Aries, a little upset from Seth’s ignorance, replies, “Even still, you idiot, did you ever think of where the light is coming from? Either way, it has to be a source,” he says as he violently yanks his finger back towards the location of the sword. More angels continue to fall unconscious to its power as Seth, offended, replies, “If this is true, then you need to cancel your last order so that we may save our brothers.” Aries slowly lowers his finger again and replies, “There’s no need. They are not strong enough to escape this trap, like us. Their fates are inevitable. Our fates are not,” he says as he turns his back towards them. “What do you mean inevitable fates,” Seth asks?

“Listen, both of you. Our fates are not sealed because we control our actions. That means we are in control of what paths we walk and the power we gain. Our brothers, on the contrary, only answer to orders. In other words, their paths are chosen by their superiors. Meaning that they are not capable of escaping, but we are. Azrael, you are our only hope,” Aries ends as he watches Michael disappear into the horizon. At this moment he knows that it’s no hope in catching up with him, and that Lucifer’s fate is foreseeable. He also notices that there are only a few hundred of his brothers left when Azrael replies, “And why is that.”

Aries raises his hand and screams out to the army, "Belay my last, brothers. We are trapped inside of a barrier created by Michael, and we have to work together to escape it." Seth interrupts, "But I thought you said..."

Aries continues as he looks at Seth with deceiving eyes, "Quiet. I have a plan to get us out of here." Azrael still looking for an answer repeats, "Why is that, Aries. How am I the only hope?" "Well if you both would let me finish, you would know. Azrael, your powers allow you to absorb the essence of life itself. Am I right," he asks while turning towards Azrael? Azrael responds, "That's right." Aries continues, "Good. Take note, and do not interrupt."

He turns back towards the army and commands, "Listen up everyone. There's no way that we will escape this barrier if we continue to work separately. You all need to jump with all your might at the same time on my command, because it only seems to attack us when we jump. However, I don't believe it can attack us all at the same time with the same strength. But remember, this is our only chance to escape it," he quickly leans back towards Azrael and Seth while the army takes position, and continues, "Now that I know what situation we're in, I know how to defeat it. This is the power of war. Just because we're in here doesn't mean that we can't fight from in here. We can't leave, but your powers can. So here's the plan. Seth, I want you to try your hardest to confuse the enemy's spirit and bring chaos amongst them. However, this will hopefully weaken the beam transference only. This is where your power comes in at, Azrael. I want you to absorb all the life that you possibly can out of those beams to weaken them even further. At the same time, do the same for Michael's sword, the enemy, and even our own brothers after they jump because they're not going to make it anyway. You will grow powerful enough to weaken the sword for only a few seconds. I'm sure of it. The flickering of the beams of light will be the sign of weakness. At this moment I shall give the order for them to jump. Immediately after they are struck you add them to your list of life forces. This will give us enough time to escape," he concludes. Seth replies, "Sounds like a plan to me." Azrael agrees, "Me too."

Without wasting time, they both put their powers to use again, but this time with more focus. Seth touches his temple areas and concentrates, while Azrael raises his hands to begin the absorption process.

In the meantime, Uriel begins to slowly lose focus on the transfer because something feels like it's invading his spiritual energy. This is Seth's power confusing them just enough so that they won't realize what's actually going on. Uriel breaks his concentration and looks around at the others to see if they are losing focus as well. To no surprise they are, and even one angel falls over from fatigue. This is a sign of Azrael also doing an excellent job without them realizing it. Uriel speaks, "What's wrong here? Why are you guys losing focus? We have to remain strong enough for only a few more moments at least. Then it'll be done," he says as many more angels lose life energy and drop their swords. Uriel gets upset and yells, "Stand up and stand strong. Our faiths dictate our strengths, and we didn't come all this way to give up now. If we found our faiths once, we can easily maintain it," he stops in the middle of his sentence due to one of his brothers falling next to him on the left. He looks down and then says, "Not you too, brother." He quickly lowers his guard and kneels down to provide aid to him. Since Uriel is the strongest one out of the group, the moment he lowers his sword, the beam begins to flicker. He doesn't realize until now that he failed a test of faith, along with the fallen, by dropping his guard, but it's too late.

To Aries, flickering is the signal to jump, and so he commands with his hands in the air, "All of you jump. For freedom!" Without hesitation the whole group jumps, excluding Seth, Azrael, and Aries. The sword sends out hundreds of energy streaks in all directions to immobilize their spirits. However, the power required to disable them all causes the weak transfer beam to dissipate with the help of Azrael's power, and then discharges, with the energy of just the sword alone. As instructed, Azrael begins to feed on the life forces of his own brothers while growing stronger twice as fast. He immediately brings his hands together and absorbs the same amount of energy from the sword that he drew from the beams of energy, the enemy, and his brothers. This creates equilibrium in power from the sword and his strength, and neutralizes the field exactly as Aries predicted. It also prevents him from damaging his spirit by using up to much of his own energy.

Aries hurriedly says, “Go now before it revitalizes.” Seth, Azrael, and Aries retreat while their brothers lie unconscious and nearly lifeless as Uriel and the others watch. One unknown angel of the Army of God asks, “It's only three of them, Uriel. Should we capture them?” Uriel replies, “No. Let them go because they have lost. We will return as Michael has surely done, and report the news of our failures as well as theirs. We have much to learn about maintaining the faith,” he ends as they all head back to Himil.

Conversely, Michael arrives at the throne and positions Lucifer, comatose, in the kneeling position at my feet for judgment of his sins. I slowly lean forward to place my hand on his head. In the process, Michael kneels, on the left hand side of Lucifer, and then stares at him as if he wanted to scream...

Chapter 5: "So, Wake Up, Wajolebe,"

I knew you would still be listening to me, Wajolebe. For your patience I will answer your next obvious question. "What happened next?" However, I need you to listen and picture what I'm about to describe to you very closely and as accurate as your faith will allow. Then I will proceed with the story. Let me start by asking you this. Do you remember everything I've said up to this point? That's very good, son. Well, prepare yourself to be a little confused for a small moment. However, I'll do my best to keep you from misunderstanding my words. You can even write all of this down if you have to. Oooh, I see. You've been doing so already, have you? Great. Let me see what you have. Hmm, I'm amazed. You even have it organized into chapters and paragraphs. That's very good, Wajolebe. I anticipated greatness from you, but you've exceeded my expectations. Well now, I guess you can continue by writing this.

Everything that I've spoken to you, starting from apparently chapter one paragraph six of your outstanding manuscript, is from the visions of Satan's spirit. This is where you might get a little confused though. So listen closely. When I placed my hand on Satan's head, I decoded his spirit. First, let me explain this concept for you in human terms. I gave you a brain and a heart, Wajolebe. In other words, you have a soul and a spirit.

In one hand is your soul. It allows you to think and choose, and it even sends signals to your mouth to speak what you think and choose. The soul characterizes who you are to you and every other human, allowing you to choose to remember or even change what you deem necessary. In the other hand is your spirit. This is the life of all your bodily functions, including your soul. It unquestionably records every action and spoken word throughout the period of your life. It's like your own personal lifetime stenographer typing everything that you do and say. When the day comes that I finally touch your spirit, I will re-live everything that you've done and said, whether you remember or not, and judge you on it. So, you'll need to learn how to combine the power of your soul and spirit very soon. For example, if you Will to live your spirit righteous, then your book of spirit records it as such and you shall be judged the same. But if you Will to live a heart of sin, then your book of heart will condemn you per se. In short, each person's spirit is a book of life, where everything is written and nothing is forgotten. Don't worry, Wajolebe. Since you're writing this all down, you'll understand what I've spoken if you keep reading it.

Use it wisely, because when the time comes you'll know exactly what the book of life is and what it means. And you'll know that the testimony inside is what you chose to bear witness to. However, in regards to Satan, he's only a spirit like all the other angels. You said it, Wajolebe! Everything from their thoughts, actions, words, and things not meant for human understanding, is recorded in spirit because they have no soul. Unlike you, they can never forget. The simple fact that they know I exist and what lies at the end of this journey requires it to be written this way, and calls for either a more strict punishment or a greater reward in the end. That's why Satan and his demons envy you. They feel that humans have everything. Even an advantage in judgment at the end. What they don't realize is that all life will be judged accordingly. It's the same as, what weighs more; a fifty pound bag of feathers or a fifty pound bag of gold? By answering this question, I know you understand, and I'll do no further explaining on this subject. This leaves me to now answer your question, Wajolebe. "What happened next?" Grab some more paper, because what's next is my word.

As time passes, I finally remove my hand from Satan's head and sit back on the throne. I'm disappointed in the vision that I gathered from within his spirit. As I lean back, Michael stands back up while Uriel and the others finally make it back. However, Uriel walks into the room alone and asks, "What should we do now, father," he drops his head as though he let me down. I reply with a reassuring smile, "Go back, with the army, and gather up all of Satan's followers, and return them here beside their master," ending as I point to an area on the right hand side of Satan.

Uriel immediately exits and informs the others. Michael remains at the foot of the throne waiting for his instructions as well. I acknowledge his wait by saying, "I want you to remain right here beside me, Michael. When he awakes and I finally assign judgment to him and his spawns, you will be the one to carry it out the sentence. Understood," I ask? Michael smiles, nods his head while placing his hands behind his back, and waits for the inevitable.

Meanwhile as the army nearly concludes the gathering of the fallen, Satan awakens, still in the kneeling position, and looks to his left only to see Michael's right leg next to his head. He flinches and grunts despicably, and immediately turns his head to the right to reject the sight. Despite the fact that he's still weary from battle and a bit dazed, he quickly deciphers the present situation and slowly looks straight ahead.

As he hatefully sets eyes on me, I say, "Finally awake, I see. And still full of such hate," I state. Satan replies with no remorse, "You damn right I am. And I will not withdraw my statement, father, or whatever you claim you are," he announces with emphasis. As I begin to speak his judgment, the army returns with his followers and places them at his right side while is say, "Damned is correct, Satan. This intense hate that you possess will escort you to that fate, and since you have no intentions of altering your beliefs, I'll waste no time in issuing your judgment," I reach out with my right hand to his unconscious supporters and continue as I notice that Aries, Azrael, and Sethrael are not present. "And there will be no chance for those who have pledged an eternity of service to such hate until that time comes. Awaken and arise," I declare as energy releases from my hands to revive them. I then proceed to issue their punishments by saying, "You will all endure the same judgment as your master. This will include the three that are trying to elude judgment. Satan, I have seen this abomination of man that you have given the rights to procreate. It too will suffer in your likeness."

Satan looks at Michael in response to what I've stated and says, "See, Michael. How can your father be so good, almighty, and perfect when innocent creations that have caused no harm to the spirit will be destroyed? This in itself is a flaw. Can't you see that," he ends trying to play his last card of deceit? Michael does not acknowledge his response and has no intentions of responding, so I continue, "Your words have no meaning in my kingdom anymore, Satan. And for your knowledge, I will not lay a hand on your creations. You will. You and your demons shall be cast out of Himil down to Eden, and will most likely cause the demise of every disgraceful creation of your own from impact. As for the future of Eden, after your collision, there will most definitely be a cloud of darkness over it. I will wipe away that cloud and continue with my plan of what I intended it to be. If there are any of your so called humans that survive your wrath, they'll then be known as primitive to all of the future life on Eden, and will therefore not be able to procreate with my own. They will depend on the hand of their idol to survive. This is the fate that you have given them," I continue as I'm suddenly interrupted by an outburst from Satan.

"You cannot. You have no rights over them or me. If you give me an eternity, then I will spend that eternity making you pay for what you have spoken. You will regret this moment in time. I promise you that," he tries to continue as I silence him by reaching out and waving my left hand from right to left once. His mouth instantly closes shut. I then leave my hand out to maintain the silence as his spirit collapses from the power. I continue, "Since you have become your own sinful master and knowingly defied me, you shall then suffer an eternity in your own Kingdom...," I pause and then continue, "...of Hell with your demons, and therefore no longer will be accepted into the Kingdom of Heaven. And any spirit foolish enough to follow your lead from then until will bear the same fate. You will not be able to escape your kingdom because there will be a key. I will place this key in Michael's possession," I end the judgment by releasing the hold of silence and creating the key in my right hand. Michael steps forward, takes a hold of the key with his left hand, absorbs it in his spirit, and prepares to carry out the sentence.

Satan continues his wordplay as soon as I release the hold, "You're making a big mistake by letting me go. I will only get stronger, and then it'll be too late for you. I will curse your seed as you have done mine and take their will. And then I will use them against you. You are all idiots," he continues as he looks around. "And you will all perish under my rule," he ends. Temporarily, he regains enough strength to stand, but Michael is prepared and says, "Satan, I will become the hands of the Almighty, and cast you and your minions out of my father's home," Michael announces as he turns and grabs Satan by the throat with his right hand. His left hand feeds off of the spiritual energy of my own and grows to an immeasurable size. Satan begins to choke from the intense crushing power of Michael's grip, quickly transforms form back and forth, and gags the words, "Do it, Michael. We're all just pawns in this game anyway," he ends while sneakily absorbing Michael spiritual essence with his right hand. Michael smiles thinking that Satan is trying to regain his power, and replies, "Be gone." With these words, he hurls Satan with an unspeakable force out of Himil and down to his creations.

While he's falling he whispers to himself, "You so easily forget that I'm the God of deception. I have already taken your precious key from up under you nose, Michael. Huh! And now that

I have seen and touched it, there will be a copy made in case you want to retrieve the original," he laughs hysterically as he begins to burn within a dark, as in pitch black, flame while falling. Michael then looks at Satan's demons without knowing that the key has been stolen, and says, "You are his followers, right? Well then, follow him," he ends aggressively as he sweeps his hand, now a size greater than the whole army, through the group like a slingshot and launches all of them out of Himil with one swipe. Screaming, they all take a fiery fall with their master towards Eden uncontrollably.

Michael turns around to face me and asks, "What should I do about the other three, father?" I reply to him, "You will leave them be. They will suffer the same fate, but as of now, their gifts will backfire and bring death and chaos of war amongst anything that is touched by the hands of Satan. They will no longer have control over it, but they will be liable for it. This is hell within itself," I end. Michael speaks about what I have just spoken, "After you have recreated the key, then how will Satan be able to touch it or anything else if he's locked in Hell, father?" I lean over and reply to him, "Because he has the key, son." Michael searches and realizes that the key is gone while I continue, "However, do not lose faith for this simple matter. I will create the proper seed as planned that he will now have access to corrupt, but there will be a separate garden to the east of Eden that no pure evil spirit will have access to. So waist no time worrying because one day I will send you to retrieve the key and soon thereafter will be his end," I conclude. Michael bows gracefully and exits.

As Satan an his demons continue their fall and enter the galaxy known as the Milky Way, him and some of the others pass by a few planets just missing them by inches at velocity that immediately placed them in an orbit, but finally collide with four additional ones; three of the largest and one which is the smallest out of twelve. With the speed and strength in which Michael hurled them, they destroy three of them on impact, and the smallest one is repositioned at the edge of the galaxy and is now placed in orbit. This leaves only seven visible planets from Eden, and one too far to be seen for the time being. They were all placed in an orbit based on how many angels passed by, how close they got to each one, and the speed at which they passed. The other three planets are shattered into thousands of different pieces and the force behind the destruction forms huge rings of rocks and dust right in the middle of your solar system.

Two of these planets are hit from an angle with such great might that it causes three fourths of these planets to be destroyed leaving behind only a small round portion of both. These excess rocks and dust created that ring I recently spoke of, also known as asteroids. The other separate pieces are identified as meteoroids. Both are placed in an orbit. The other planet that I created with different elements, such as ice, water, and rock is also shattered and added to this ring; however, some parts remain ice and water, and are sent into an orbit. This orbit is separate from the asteroid's orbit and has a trail of evaporating water and other molecules that resembles a tail.

Other pieces of these planets, including the dust from them, are propelled towards the outside planets with the help of enormous gravitational pulls from the larger ones, and forms rings of dust and rock around them as well. Some are even big enough to distinguish themselves as planet sized rocks that are orbiting a larger planet, and therefore not considered as such. To top it all off, Satan passes within the flames of the sun and reaches out to grab a hold of anything that. To no avail, he keeps passing through because the sun is not solid where he expects it to be. The speed at which he travels sets the sun in a very slow rotation, and the fire that already surrounds him as he falls is intensified a thousand times over. The blaze now surrounding him is quickly corrupted by his evil spirit, as well as anything he eventually controls, and turns dark in resemblance to his essence. This will be added to further his punishment and this new flame will greet him when he reaches his kingdom in Hell.

Without a doubt, the different collisions slow their decent towards Eden, however many of them surpassed Satan and the others. These demons will most definitely collide with Eden first. Nevertheless, it is still all of their destinations in general, and so no obstacle will cease their descent except Eden. As Satan continues to fall, the darkness from the mighty pitch-black flames become visible from the surface of Eden.

Now let me explain something to you, Wajolebe. I'm sure that this spectacle is probably hard for your mind to imagine, so again I will do my best to clarify it until you understand it. It's very important that you do. As a matter of fact, since you have been so attentive, I'll do something better than explaining it to you. I will allow you to see it first hand. What's wrong, Wajolebe? You looked worried now. Well, you needn't be. Your faith is strong, and you will not be harmed by darkness because of it. As long as you remain confident, I will be with you and continue this line of communication between us. Yes, this means that I am going to leave you physically, but I'll remain by your side spiritually. However you do have a choice to make. Which way would you rather preserve our communication; physically, mentally, or spiritually? This is your choice, so choose. Take your time because this will determine your fate. Good, you have chosen wisely, Wajolebe. However, remember this.

The decision that you have made is the hardest to manage and the most challenging. But as you have faith in me, I also have faith in you. From this moment on, I have nothing further to teach you. You are now ready to face this evil that I speak of without fear. I am going to send your spirit to Eden and allow you to see through the eyes of a primate of what happens next. This is the best way to clarify the details. Now lean your head forward, Wajolebe, and let me touch your spirit. Close your eyes and listen for your name. When you hear it called again, restore your sight and you will become. Take note of what you witness, for this will be the first of many times with you that I'll allow sight in this manner. Translate what you see and speak it to the masses when the time arrives. Fear not what the outcome may be, for it is already written. And fear not what others may say about what you have witnessed because they have not seen it at all. For you are wise, and you will always remain as such, providing you believe. Now, journey out towards Eden and prepare to open your eyes straight ahead. Thereafter, you'll become the narrator and speak as yourself with the guidance of all that's holy, and no one, not even Satan himself, will ever cease your voice and knowledge because you are...

Wajolebe, "My name! I heard my name," I say to myself quickly opening my eyes as I was instructed to do straight ahead. The Almighty had already positioned me in the proper manner for what he wanted me to see first. Right away I notice the time of day. The sun is, "Directly above me," I ask myself out loud realizing that I can't understand a single word that I'm speaking? As I continue to focus straight ahead, there's nothing but a flat surface of white sand that continues past my line of sight.

From this point I promptly scan the flat terrain while taking mental notes as I turn my head. To my right I see huge trees and vegetation, about a quarter of a mile or more, that stand at least seventy to eighty feet high. These trees and plant life consist of a wide variety of colors, and within them seems to be different animals roaming about making strange noises as they move. They seem to be giants as well, at least from what I can see and hear in the distance.

Also, a majority of what I see looks abnormal too, exactly like the descriptions. However, to my left is more sand, and in the horizon appears to be an enormous body of water. This may just be an ocean, but I'm not for sure because of how far it is away. By the looks of it, it would probably take me an hour or more to reach it by foot if that was my purpose. But it's not, so I continue my visual search by looking behind me, and what I see is what I expected. More sand! I was either on the coastline of a prehistoric beach, or I was on a miniature desert surrounded by water and plant life. Anyhow, I begin to kneel down to pick up some sand, but two things catch my attention right away. First, I spot a stick of some sort, about the size of half my arm length and width, lying on the sand in front of me. Second, to my surprise, I notice myself. I'm covered with a large amount of grayish-black hair from feet to head. Detecting this makes me examine my entire body from front to back in amazement. The only thing that I don't have the luxury of seeing is my face. So I slowly raise my hands and take a mental note of what I feel. "I guess this is what a primate is, huh," I ask out loud to myself?

However, something draws my attention back to the stick on the ground. It's odd that this is the only stick in my view but, "Maybe this is what I should use to record what I see," I think to myself. As I reach out to pick it up, I come to realize something else. There's a pattern or symbol of some sort encircling me in the sand that I didn't see from the standing position. It's barely visible from where I'm looking at now and it doesn't seem to harm me in any way. I actually feel as though it'll protect me from harm if any dangerous situation arises. In any case, I'm not going to step outside the boundaries of it until necessary, but for now I need to be taking notes.

So, I pick up the stick and begin drawing what I've seen so far in this strange world of Eden. "First, I'll sketch a mini version of the symbol just outside the lines of the one beneath me to signify my location on this Jurassic desert, beach, or whatever it is. Then, I'll expand the picture outwards in relations to what I have seen so far around me. My plan is to draw everything that I observe once I start to venture out of my current position into this unknown world.

If I have to depict an image on every rock, cave, or tree to represent everything else that I see on my journey, then so be it. This is what my purpose is and what I've been informed to do," I say proudly.

While I'm in the middle of sketching this symbol, from what I can see of it, something bizarre happens. The symbol begins to glow with a white shade and blends with the sand. Then it goes from a light orange to a bright red color. This weird incidence has me believing that maybe I'm doing something wrong. Now that I'm thinking about it, I can barely see the original symbol. Perhaps I'm not drawing the same one. Maybe the one that I'm drawing is evil because, "Something just doesn't seem right about that at all," I say out loud. Immediately a voice in my head tells me not to worry. "Have faith," It says as the sound of the word faith echoes out. Without worry, I continue to draw the symbol by taking quick glances at the original to make sure it's as accurate as possible, or at least sketch what I can see. As I continue, I hear that voice again, but this time it says, "Remember the sight to behold."

"That's right. The Almighty spoke of the darkness from the mighty pitch black flames becoming on Eden. It's not meant for me to be harmed, I guess, as long as I stay within the confines of this symbol. But I haven't noticed anything strange in the sky, except that the sun is directly above me, and it causes a weird gravitational pull on Eden. Maybe it controls the way things happen here right now," I conclude my thoughts while concentrating on the sun as I complete the last line in the symbol. I can actually tell that the sun is shining on all of Eden at once, and that it stays in the same spot all the time because there's no moon. Other than that, there's still nothing unusual happening in the sky at the moment. However, there is something happening on the ground though. It's beginning to softly and slowly vibrate in odd sequences. "It's obviously not an earthquake," I say to myself.

I try to stand up with the stick in my right hand, but the symbol that I drew glows brighter and locks the branch it in place. So I try to let go of it, but strangely enough, I can't let go either. "What's going on here," I ask out loud while looking around? I keep trying to pull away from the small symbol so that I can get my whole body back inside of the safe zone, but the more I tug, the more Eden vibrates like it's mimicking my pull. I immediately look back up at the sky because the vibration is accompanied by a constant thunderous sound. To no surprise, nothing is happening up there, but as I look towards the horizon, there's a cloud of dust gathering. "I'm definitely not a genius, but my idea of an approaching dust cloud accompanied by vibrations and thunder would be a stampede. And I really wouldn't want to be in the way of that" I nervously think.

I continue to try to break free from this strange hold, but it does me no good. I'm beginning to get a little nervous now because I actually see thousands of animals charging in my direction in the distance. It's so many of them that they're stretched across the whole horizon, and to make the situation worse, the ones in the trees to my right are getting terrified too. I even notice more primates like myself running away from the forest. That's when it all happens. I look up one more time directly into the sun. But something is wrong. "How can there be a black spot in the middle of the sun," I think to myself as I continue to struggle? To give you a clear picture of what this looks like, the sun is about the size of your average car tire and the spot is about the size of a dime, and it's growing incredibly fast. That's when I start to notice more of them appearing all over the sky in the distance, but much closer and fiery red like, "The symbol. The same color as the symbol. It was warning me of this," I scream out loud.

I really begin to struggle now because the stampede is only a few hundred yards away, trees are tumbling over, and I can't get to safety. However, just when I think that the situation can't get any worse, one of those fiery red objects break the clouds over the water to my left, disappears on the horizon, and impacts with the force of a major earthquake from what seems to be hundreds or maybe thousands of miles away. My instinct tells me that those animals are running from a previous crash of which I couldn't see, or their animal instincts forewarned them of something terrible arriving. "That's got to be what it is. Otherwise why would they be running away," I ask myself while barely shaking my head back and forth confusingly. At that distance, I'm pretty sure it'll be a tidal wave of some sort coming my way soon, but right now I'm worried about being trampled. So I turn to look back straight ahead, and weird looking animals finally start rushing and scrambling over and past me in all directions. Some of the smaller ones are getting crushed in the process along with the big ones getting knocked over, but somehow I'm surviving this disaster. "I guess the symbol is my protection as long as I believe while I'm inside of it," I say.

It's getting dark so fast now that any soul can tell that it's unnatural. Dust is covering the air in massive amounts, so much that it's becoming barely visible. All the animals finally pass by and luckily no tidal wave as of yet, but I'm still in the same spot unable to move. All I can do is witness what's going on. That's when it hit me. "That's what Alpha wanted. This is only the first of many times that I'll be allowed 'the sight' in this manner. It is only meant for me to witness and record," I say to myself.

At this moment I am instantly released from the symbol's hold, and I'm granted sight beyond the dust cloud. I begin to see more of these fiery red objects raining down from the sky and colliding with Eden far away from my location. Most of these objects look like the size of an average giant person, but all in all probably causing significant damage by most likely killing animals and vegetation. The other fireballs look like they may be huge debris from the heavens. I slowly stand to my feet, wobbling from each impact, to witness the most unforgettable sight a soul would ever witness.

The sun is now completely extinguished by that dark figure, and is somehow moving in the opposite direction. "Instead of straight up, it's now halfway between it's last point and the horizon. "That's weird," I say out loud. As more of the fireballs collide with Eden, I begin to figure out that they are slowly but surely knocking Eden off of its perfect axis and causing it to shift, but not rotate. And the impacts are pushing it further away from the sun as well. This is only the beginning too. "If I'm correct about these fireballs, then they're not fireballs at all. They're the demons expelled from heaven, and are most likely accompanied by chunks of leftover planets that they destroyed on the way. "If that's true, then this large dark aura masking the sun is none other than Satan himself," I speak with certainty as something runs past me in the direction that the animals were running in. I suspect that it may have been a demon, but it was excessively fast and it's still too murky out to verify it. But if it was a demon, then, "Where is he running to," I say out loud?

Approximately thirty seconds or less has passed so far since the first visual impact. "This is all happening way too fast," I think to myself. As I turn back, I see the dark figure drawing closer to Eden. The sun is completely extinguished and I can't tell where it's located any longer because black flames are stretched from the right to the left edges of the earth covering it up. Surprisingly enough, the outline of the flames are highly visible in darkness itself. "Well, that confirms it. This is Satan and his demons because only he is damned to be seen as the shadows in the darkness," I say under my breath as something runs by me again, this time towards the forest. I think I caught a glimpse of if this time, but I'm still not certain.

The ground begins to shake again, but this time a gale force wind follows it, along with tons of rubbish. The wind is actually the shock wave arriving from the first impact in a little less than a minute followed by, "My God," I say astonishingly as my eyes follow the path of the enormous tidal wave! It looks to be well over a mile high, and it demolishes everything in its path except for me of course. A few seconds pass and the mayhem appears to be over. However, the whole thing is only beginning. I turn my head back in the direction that the wave originated from. The landscape has dramatically changed. The flat surface of white sands has been completely reformed and populated with wet dunes. I'm able to see them because the blast of wind has cleared most of the air in the immediate affected areas.

"What is this," I ask out loud? The top of the sun is barely visible on the horizon just above the black flames, and it looks like a normal sunset. "Is this the first sunset," I ask myself? No sooner than I ask that, I see the gigantic black flames disappear under the horizon as Satan descends to Eden. "If there are any of those strange looking animals left, then soon it won't be because I believe that Satan is about to collide with the southern portion of Eden," I say out loud. The segment that I'm speaking of will be better described as the South Pole, even though it's not a pole as of yet. The black flames and the fire from his descent become so intense even from the opposite end of the planet, that a vast amount of sand where I stand in random areas is instantly converted to an off-green colored glass. The color comes from the instant evaporation of water from sand to glass, and will probably never be duplicated under normal circumstances again.

Many of Satan's minions collide with Eden just seconds before he does burning, shattering, and expelling this green glass substance across Eden. Their collisions cause numerous small eruptions to occur. Then the main event happens. I hear a sound that I believe will never be heard by man again, and it's the sound of Satan crashing to Eden. The impact sets of a chain reaction of numerous volcanic eruptions throughout all of Eden. The energy generated from the collision alone is so great that it immediately drives out a portion of the planet, tilts the axis, and sets Eden into an elliptical orbit. The sound of the impact alone would kill a person. I actually see this enormous portion of Eden from a distance literally driven out, propelled into space, and set in motion around the planet in regards to its gravitational pull. However it doesn't spin because of how it's ejected outwards in a straight line. Trillions of tons of magma burns, dries, and falls from the surface of it as it exits the atmosphere in what seems to be a second or less. What I can't see at the moment is how Pangaea is no longer one large landmass, but has been crumbled into different terrains that are now slowly inching away from each from the impact.

"In...Crrreeedible," I yell out, and then pause before I continue! "I think I just witnessed the birth of the moon." An enormous excess of lava immediately begins to get sucked into the core of Eden as if gravity was pulling it in through the hole that was created by the impact. Water follows afterwards while evaporating at the same time. I'm not a hundred percent positive, but I'm sure that this is the point where Eden begins its first revolution around the sun. Everything for as far as my eyes can see at this moment, seems to be disintegrated. But the moment doesn't last long. Without delay, once again the sky is darkened and covered with smoke, debris, and soot. By the looks of it, this phenomenon will be like this for eons.

It remains pitch black for only a few seconds because the skies are being lit up by volcanic eruptions and fire storms all over. "This is truly the sight of Armageddon," I think out loud. I look down at the symbol again since I'm beginning to feel the heat below my feet, and to my surprise it's glowing similar to the color of the lava. "Is this a sign to step away from it," I question myself. At this moment, something dashes by my left side. As I turn to catch a glimpse of what I think it is, something sprints past my right side before I get a chance to completely twist. I immediately look to my right and set eyes on a demon fleeing on all fours. Its body is covered with weird markings similar to the symbol below, and they're all shifting in a circular pattern. Each one is on fire reflecting the same light as the magma. "Well then, I guess that is what scurried past me earlier. But how could they still be conscious after their landings," I ponder as something even more strange comes to my attention. "Not only is it running, but it looks afraid of something too," I take note as curiosity gets the better of me.

I quickly turn to see why it's running away so frantically, but I observe nothing in the immediate vicinity. Everything up close is easy to see from the light of the fire and molten rock, but objects closer to the horizon are impossible to distinguish. With this I grow more inquisitive and decide to step away from the symbol to jog in the path from which the demon was coming from. The first irrelevant thing I notice is how funny I'm running. But besides that, the symbol's protection completely slips my mind as I proceed in the opposite direction for approximately one minute. Astonishingly, I'm not harmed by anything, but I feel every aspect of the current situation. At this point, Satan is the only thing flowing through my mind, but something isn't adding up right. "I mean because, why would they be running from their leader if that's actually what they're running from. Maybe they're afraid that Satan will punish them because they failed to win the war," I say under my breath as I pick up the pace. The theory makes hardly any since, so I disregard it.

While I continue to advance forward, I notice a weird barrier moving in the distance from different areas heading towards me. My first instinct is magma flow because of the continuous volcanic eruptions all around me. Though, it could be a horde of demons headed this way running from the same thing. However, it's hard to tell because I can't make any type of distinction from this distance or from the vibrations. Whatever it is, it's moving rapidly. As I draw closer, it finally hits me that I'm not in the safe zone any longer, and more importantly, "That's definitely not magma coming my way. Those are demons," I say nervously as I stop in my tracks quickly analyzing how far they're advancing this fast. I hastily look back in the direction of the symbol hoping that I can make it back in time. But by the looks of it, I won't because from the time I first noticed them that far until now seem to be fifteen seconds or more. And from that distance, they would have to be moving at super fast speeds to get this far that quickly. "I'm not going to make it," I think to myself. Nevertheless, I don't waste anytime worrying about it too much. Right away I turn and sprint towards the symbol, but as I thought, it is too late.

As I continue to backtrack at full speed, demons are fleeing close by me in all directions. My body now begins to manifest and solidify into an actual primate. "I'm becoming real," I say perplexingly as I slow my pace and begin to focus on the palm of my hands. "I should've stayed where I was," I think. A demon coming up behind at a high speed bumps my right shoulder as I fade in, and continues to run straight through me as I fade out. The collision causes me to stumble over, but hardly knocks him off course. However, he does look back to see what he hit and continues to run without caring. I hit the ground and roll forward a couple of times before I actually spring back into action without hesitation. "There it is," I pronounce as I get closer to the symbol. I cautiously look over my left shoulder, while they're still herding past me, trying to avoid another collision. Unfortunately, I notice that I may get ran over by another one heading my way.

I turn my head back towards the symbol and realize that it's fading away very fast, and for good this time. "I'm too close for it to disappear on me," I think impetuously. As I continue to materialize it continues to fade concurrently, so I make a rash decision to dive for it. "Aahh," I scream as I leap forward as hard as I can. It's almost like everything instantaneously decelerates to slow motion as I fall. At this point, four things happen. First, the symbol is fading to extinction. It's actually disappearing faster than I'm falling, and I'm only a few feet from landing on it or near it. Second, my primate form becomes more concrete to Eden as the symbol vanishes. This is the phase where I begin to fear the almost certain outcome. Next, the heat from the lava is growing to be extremely blistering because of my increasing physicality. So hot that if I touch the ground without the symbol being there at all, I fear that I will burn to a crisp even though the lava is not directly beneath me. Finally, the demon behind me is merely a second away from causing another collision on all fours. He's so close that his head is right at the heel of my left foot.

To no surprise, the demon's head does connect with my foot, but plays in my favor. Instead of knocking me off course as I feared it would, the impact in fact impels me forward the required distance causing me to flip backwards while I'm moving forward. He runs directly under me and looks up in my eyes as I rotate the full three hundred and sixty degrees. "Ooof," I verbalize as I fall flat on my stomach releasing whatever air that I have left in my lungs. Breathless and in pain, without wasting time I position my arms and hands to get up to continue towards the symbol without even lifting my head. However, as I hoist myself up, I notice that I am within the boundaries of the symbol and it's fully visible to me again. In spite of this fortunate incident, what happens next is terrifying.

The demon that low bridged me stops in his tracks, inquisitively turns around, and comes back to find out what he saw while the others continue to flee. I remain silent and motionless as he approaches the symbol. I start to think to myself, "I wonder if he can see me." He gradually initiates a sniff and search in the area that we made eye contact. He continues until he bumps his head on the outside of the barrier in which the symbol has created for my protection. The fact that he can't see what's there makes him frustrated. As a result he rams the unseen barrier with his left shoulder blade and continues to try infringing it. After a couple of seconds of this behavior, the barricade scarcely gives off a blue glow, which he can see, and causes him to pause.

At this point, I'm one hundred percent positive that he can make out at least a ghostly imagine of my figure. Sure enough, he begins slowly but angrily looking up from feet to head tracing every inch of my almost invisible image on the way. He finally makes eye contact with me for the second time, raises his right hand as he stands completely up, and speaks something in an unknown language. He starts to take a swing at me in the middle of his speech, but something else grabs his attention during his attempt. He dreadfully looks around me to the left, and promptly turns around and retreats with the remainder of the pack in an all out panic. I follow him with my eyes trying not to move until the blue glow disappears. "Whew...," I sigh in relief that he's gone, pause to calm my nerves, and then continue to speak softly, "...I believe he actually saw me. Thank God the barrier was stronger than he was. But what was he saying," I end, not realizing that he was saying I was not one of them.

A sudden silence falls over the scorching planet, and all I hear are the flames from the fires burning behind me, mainly concentrating specifically in the area where the moon separated. Even the vibrations from the eruptions cease. I heed this as a warning and turn to see what's happening. I focus my visuals as far as I can see which is maybe one hundred feet and declining every second in tandem with Eden's deterioration state. This, however, doesn't prevent me from seeing a strange motion that's darker than pitch black near the horizon increasing in elevation above the ground. First, what looks like a massive right arm is feeling around and trying to grab a hold of something. It's so dark that the light from the magma surrounding it and falling off of it in the nearby vicinity is visible from where I stand. Right away, I know exactly what's transpiring. "Dark within darkness can only mean one thing...Satan," I say under my breath.

Next, I see the other arm come out a grab the edge. He's so enormous that I'm able to hear the sound of his hands pounding the ground along with huge rocks striking each other as if they're falling down a cliff. More lava becomes evident as his head begins to slowly but surely rise up over his shoulders. So much that it emphasizes the outline of his dark physical structure. He's obviously hauling some of the same materials that flowed into the crater earlier, back to the surface as he emerges. "Uuhhh," he grunts extensively loud for about one and a half seconds. His voice echoes within this silent moment and causes a weird ringing in my ears similar to the sound of a fork scraping a plate. "Aahh," I enunciate as I irritably cover my ears. The minute the ringing stops, the planet springs back to life with the sounds of eruptions and vibrations. As I continue to look ahead, I see Satan completely pull himself out of the aperture. He had descended to Eden on the Southern portion so fast and hard that the impact pushed him through to the Northern region, and now he's scaled his way out of it.

He begins to gradually move closer towards my location in an injured manner while moaning and grunting as he advances. Each step seems to equal nearly a mile or so due to his size. This means that my location is may be approximately fourteen or fifteen steps away. I can't express enough how enormous he is. With four steps slowly taken, Satan begins to shout profusely while looking up, "Damn you. What makes you better than me, huh? I've proven that you're not the only one who can create life, but so too can all creations. And you, Michael, how dare you put your filthy hands on me. You all will pay. I'll see to it myself. Now that I have the key, you can't stop me," he continues to rant.

As he takes about ten more steps, he nears my vicinity and I begin to see more and more details of his physical structure through the darkness. “I hope he doesn’t see me. Please let him not see me,” I say softly. As soon as I finish speaking, I think to myself, “What am I, stupid? I should’ve thought that instead of saying it. Idiot! I hope he didn’t hear that.” From his current location, he’s probably too far to hear what said. In addition, his height will probably prevent him from hearing itty bitty me. “Wait. Why did he stop moving,” I think again to myself?

Satan speaks out, “I created all life on this planet, and all is apart of me. But, it’s something or someone hear that doesn’t belong here. I can hear it and feel it. Come out wherever you are,” he begins to scan the area where I am. I start to get a little nervous about his speech. “It’s not possible. There’s no way he heard me whisper,” I say to myself. He takes two gigantic steps which lands his right foot directly in front of the symbol. He again declares vigorously, “I said come out!” He turns from left to right continuing his search. “Hmmm. That sound came from this area. I know it’s here, but maybe I’m looking wrong,” he utters to himself.

At this point I really get nervous and begin to think, “Just keep going. It’s nothing here. Please just keep going.” No sooner than I finished thinking, Satan begins to shrink to his normal size, which is about the size of an averaged giant, so that he can get a better landscaped view. Also, at his normal size, he restores his health more rapidly. At the exact moment in which he stabilizes, my heart repeatedly skips beats. His eyes aren‘t exactly pointed in my direction, but I already know that it’s inevitable. Everything seems to become slow motion as his head turns in my direction. Immediately I kneel down to pray. “Father, I know that his eyes are much sharper than that one demon that spotted me, and he will eventually see me. Protect me, Alpha. Guide me through this forthcoming altercation. Amen,” I end as Satan’s eyes fall on me.

My chest immediately aches with anxiety as though I was shot with an arrow by means of his eyes piercing my soul. "Not only does your Alpha hear prayers, I hear your plea as well, unintelligent one," Satan proclaims. Fortunately, he doesn't completely know what he sees. To him I'm like a barely visible ghost. Nonetheless, this doesn't impede his inquisitiveness. He immediately grabs at me with his left hand but clashes with the barricade instead. "Whaat," he proclaims as he angrily steps back and looks up. "If this is another one of your lame restrictions, then I shall destroy it too," he boasts to the Almighty.

He then begins to make strange hand, arm, and leg movements resembling a fighting style. "What in God's name is he doing," I timidly think to myself. After a few more thrusts, His hands begin to emit darkness even more sinister than his own appearance while he roars a phrase that I'll never forget, "Modus operandi exposé." With that, he snickers at the exact moment he strikes the obstruction with his left hand, repeats the phrase and strikes again with his right hand so quick that I barely observe the technique. The darkness rapidly engulfs the shield causing it to reveal all of its hidden contents at the same rate. The symbol below me immediately brightens in response to Satan's actions and tries to undo the dark curse. He catches a glimpse of the glowing emblem and says, "This is my world, my playground, and your curse." He punches the ground with his left hand and sends a shockwave of darkness towards the symbol. At this point, there's nothing that I can do but pray even harder because the symbol is blanketed with darkness and the shield is breaking into pieces.

"Whatever you are, you will show yourself to me and I will obliterate you. No mercy on my terrain," Satan says with much hate! He begins to impatiently and vigorously snatch sections of the shield away directly above me until he creates an opening, and then tries to reach in and pull me out. He continues this rampage until the barricade completely collapses into thousands of pieces from all the mayhem. I continue to pray silently to the Almighty for protection while Satan grabs me by the neck with his right hand, lifts me over his head, and says, "You resemble my creation of the seed, but your life force reeks of that whom I hate the most," he pauses for two seconds. In these two seconds, we both look up to the heavens simultaneously. He looks up to spite the Almighty, but I look up to send my prayers. However I'm unable to see the sky from all the havoc, but as an alternative I hear a voice in my head say, "Even when darkness seems to prevail, the most minuscule light imaginable will be visible."

At this exact moment, I feel wonderful. Nothing at this point has any meaning except God Almighty. I close my eyes and instantly accept what's about to happen to me. Satan looks back at me and continues, "No mercy! Uuuhhaaahhh." He jolts back his left hand and advances it forward with maximum intensity. In this mere moment from contact, time slows to a halt at the exact point where I feel one of his knuckles scarcely touching a hair follicle on the lower right side of my face. Right now, I'm still watching the back of my eyelids which are beginning to remind me of an empty universe. Again I hear that same voice echoing in my eardrum, "The most miniscule light."

"Father, give me strength to defeat this beast," I continue to pray as I see a speck of light appear in the upper region behind my right eyelid. As the light intensifies, so does the echo. I open my eyes and to my surprise, the light is illuminating in the same location through all the dust and debris in the sky. Time remains idle, for the moment, as a single solid beam quickly projects from the source in a straight line towards my right eye. I try escaping from the clutch of Satan's hand around my neck to fully accept the forthcoming of this ray of light even though I have no idea what's going to happen. However, I'm locked within the grasps of time, as well, only able to move my eyes.

As my right eye absorbs the ray of light, I hear the voice say, "You now have the Eye of Sentient; The Star. Use its' power for good and there will be nothing you can't accomplish. This Star is rare when placed in the right eye, and will be uncommon from now until the end of time. You are now known as a Seer; Prophet. Time is in your hands. Persevere, my son. Teach the generations, and rebuke that which is evil," It fades out as the radiance dissipates. At any moment, I'm sure that everything will spring back to life and my jaw will be broken. "I have to do something now. Move your hands Wajolebe," I think to myself.

Without hesitation, the Star sends a visible electric current streaming from my eye to my right hand. When it reaches my hand, I'm instantly able to move my arm. I quickly reach over, grab the wrist of the hand that's squeezing my neck, and uncouple his grip. At this point I begin to fall at a snails pace, and the fist that made contact with my face, gradually makes its way up towards my cranium touching every strand of hair as I fall. All together, energy surges to my left arm as well. As soon as my head is clear of his blow, time accelerates back to normal. Satan misses his punch while I safely hit the ground.

"What," he declares astonishingly? Without hesitating, he looks down. By this time, I'm taking a full swing at his midsection with a hard right. I connect while energy surges through his stomach and causes him to slightly lean forward and grunt, "Uuuhh." Immediately I jab the same spot with a powerful electric left blow. This time he bends over clinching his stomach with both arms while proclaiming, "Aaargh." Again, without procrastinating, I jump upwards with full power and uppercut a powerful right hand strike to his chin as he bends over. The jolt of power sends him airborne, opposite of my position, while he releases a horrific cry of pain as he lands on his back. By not fully recovering from his recent battle with Michael and his impact with Eden, Satan is fully vulnerable to my newly acquired power. Otherwise, he would've found a way to easily avoid my punches and counterattack.

However, even though he's weaker than usual, "I'm not taking a chance in finding out how quick he can heal," I say to myself as I turn to escape in the reverse direction as fast as I can sprint. Of course while I'm running, my conscience is telling me to find a safe place to screen my presence, but my curiosity is indicating to glance back. After I get a few yards away, I submit to my curiosity and look back. Just then, a bolt of lightning strikes directly in the path in which I'm running and cause me to recoil in the opposite direction twisting as I fall. The blast knocks me backwards at least a couple of feet and lands me face down scarcely missing the lava flow to my right. Amazingly I'm not harmed by the heat, but it's still very hot to my skin. As I slowly lift myself off the ground, I notice Satan doing the same thing. Again, I waste no time turning around to begin my retreat. However, I notice in the location where the lightning strike hit, an object that resembles an oval shaped capsule. As I make my way over to it, Satan releases a colossal cry causing me to turn back around off of impulse.

"You will never escape me mortal. I am Satan. Hear my call," Satan exclaims while reaching up towards the dark sky. The obscurity begins to swirl like the formation of a tornado but instead quickly clears an enormous circular opening above his head. He releases a stream of shadows from each one of his fingertips into the void, sets eyes on me, and begins to laugh ungodly. The shadows resemble strings connected to a puppet, and if my instincts serve me correct, more than one. If he's doing what I think he's doing, then I really need to get out of here fast. I immediately turn around towards the object on the ground and say out loud while profusely releasing a large breath, "Please let this be something of use." I swiftly go over and give a rough examination of this entity. "It doesn't seem to be of any harm," I say to myself. I then pick the object up with my right hand and resume my retreat hastily as I continue to look back. I continue to look back over my left shoulder, and at this moment I hear Satan shout, “God of Morality, War, and Chaos come to me. Renew my strength,” he ends as he falls to his knees with his hands still in the air. I can’t see exactly what’s happening, but I presume that a door to another dimension is opening above his head.

“My instincts were correct. He’s summoning Azrael, Aries, and Seth to Eden to revitalize his power and wounds. This is very, very bad,” I exclaim. I don’t get too far before dark lightning continuously begins to strike him. His body convulses from all the surges like he’s having a seizure while his hands remain in the air, until suddenly it’s over. “Is he fully recovered now, or what,” I ask myself? He stands to his feet so fast that the movement is almost invisible to the naked eye. I make an assumption to myself when he does this, “If he can move that fast, then he’s fully recovered and can definitely catch me at will.” This is a true statement; however, my guess is that he has other motives for me. At this point he forcefully lowers his left arm, closes his fist, and commands, “God of War.”

Aries descends through the void at a rapid pace, crashes to the ground on his left knee, and replies, “At your command, my true lord.” Satan smiles while repeating the process with his right hand, and ordering, “God of Chaos.” This time Seth permeates through the cavity and impacts with a force so tremendous that it sends a shockwave past my current location. I stumble in the process from the quake, but continue to retreat while avoiding the small streams of lava near me as Seth replies, “By your leave, my lord.” After each arrival Satan regains a small portion of his strength to heal directly from his spawns essences. Without wasting time, he vigorously slams his two fists together near his chest causing a dark electric reaction, and announces in a death-defying voice, “God of Mortality, feed me the most sinister energy to unite my new establishment.”

At this exact moment, I feel myself getting warm very quickly, and then something strange occurs. The capsule in my hand becomes very cool and forces me to look at it. It's a good thing that I do too because as I turn around I notice that I'm on the brink of running full speed into a lake of lava. My right foot is actually on the edge of where the stream begins. The close encounter throws me off balance for a split second, and then I hear, "I am Azrael, God of Mortality; Lord of Death. Hear my cry," he shouts as I turn around to witness his descent after regaining my balance. From the looks of things, Azrael is the strongest of the three dark Gods.

Unlike the others, he descends very slow as dark energy is being released from him into Satan. "I'm not waiting around to see what they can do. Right now I need to find a way around this magma," I think as the pod continues to grow colder. I look to the left and right, but the lake seems to be infinite in both directions. "There's no way around it, and there's absolutely no way that I can jump it. I'm definitely not going back the other way," I continue to ponder as the container gets colder by the second. It's nearly freezing my hands at this moment, but it's not causing detriment to me in any way. "Is this thing trying to tell me something? No, it can't be. Maybe the real question is, did it just protect me from crossing paths with this lava," I start to wonder?

In reality it is trying to protect me from any potential hazards, but I have no clue of what it is and what it does at this moment. It begins to ice over and change my whole body temperature to match its likeness. This is where I realize that it may be attempting to safeguard me, and I courageously say out loud, "Well, here goes nothing." I make a step of faith with my left foot out towards the lava, and to my surprise, the exact portion of the lava below my foot congeals at an unbelievable rate. The container ices my left foot well below absolute zero and equalizes the temperature of the magma until it solidifies to rock instantaneously. A vast amount of steam is the result of this encounter between my icy foot and the hot magma.

"Well I'll be. I don't understand it, but it's doing it," I say miraculously as I immediately take another step with my right foot a little quicker, and receive the same results. I lift up my left foot to repeat the process, and as I do so, the harden lava below slowly returns to its normal temperature until it's liquefied again. "What exactly is this thing," I ask as I look at the capsule? I then turn around to observe the situation behind me one last time to ensure that the distance between us is to my advantage precisely when Azrael sets both feet on Eden.

Azrael replies, "What are your orders, my Lord," as Satan reaches his arms to the dark sky while looking up? This time the void in the dark sky spins faster and begins to funnel down towards Satan's hand like a massive tornado. Once it reaches his hands, he glares in my direction and replies to each of them while pointing at me, "Exterminate him." Without responding they begin advancing in my direction as he directs the whirlwind ahead of them. It's acting as a tracker because it's following the exact path in which I ran. In addition it's providing a cover for Satan's minions, "As if it isn't hard enough to see already. Yet and still, that's my queue," I respond as I immediately turn and run full speed over the lava. The faster I run, the more the capsule freezes my feet to protect me from the heat. After about seven seconds of sprinting, the pod begins to glow a greenish blue color brighter and brighter. I think to myself, "Is it glowing based on how fast I'm running, or is it substituting for the difference in temperatures. I've already figured out that it's protecting me, but I have a feeling that it's more to this thing than what I see. I need to figure out what these different signs mean."

At this point, the pod is nearly blinding me. I instinctively slow my pace due to visible limitations, but it continues to glow at the same intensity. I switch the capsule to my left hand only to partially block the light from my eyes with my right arm. “Well that answers that,” I say to myself, in regards to my previous question. In reality, it also answers the second question too. If it’s not glowing based on how fast I’m running, then there’s no need to substitute for the heat difference between my feet and the magma.

“Maybe I’m about to run into something else,” I think as I vigilantly slow my pace a little more to scan the area ahead, as far and as much as I can see. However, while still running at a quick rate, I see nothing harmful within a ten foot zone. Everything further than this area restricts my ability to see as a result of the blinding light and the darkness on Eden. I can’t even measure the distance that I have to run to escape this lake of lava because the pod continues to shine brighter and blind me even more. “It doesn’t matter. I have faith that it’s going to protect me,” I say out loud. As I speak, the capsule releases a shockwave, approximately the size of my palm, at a rate close to the speed of light. The jolt discharges a stream of energy that forces me to stop dead in my tracks as though I’m running towards a heavy gusting wind. As the jolt is released, the pod becomes one with my left hand.

“Whaa...What,” I nervously cry out? I begin to frantically shake my hand in hopes to disengage it, but it merges even more. “What exactly is this thing,” I ask out loud? Confused, I look back contemplating whether or not this item was sent by the Almighty or Satan, being that he is the God of Deception. He could have easily deceived me to think that it was a heavenly object. The ground quakes heavily as I turn, and as I try to see in the distance, the next quake catches me off guard sending me falling face first towards the lava. The moment I begin to fall the capsule dispels a series of shockwaves, five more to be exact, each drastically growing in diameter at a superior speed.

The first one prevents me from falling by thrusting me back to the standing position. The last four are released while expanding in sequence. In fact, the last one spreads so far that when the wave returns and fades away two feet in front of me in less than 3 seconds, it's so powerful that it clears the dust and debris from the sky allowing me to visually locate Satan and his three sidekicks. In addition, it also disposes of his so called tornado vortex. "What is this thing doing? And did that last pulse just scale the entire circumference of Eden," I ask myself not realizing that it had made a full revolution around the planet? Azrael is now only about sixty feet away, and the other two are right behind him as I quickly regain my composure to continue my retreat.

"You can't escape mortality, imprudent one. It's irrefutable," Azrael shouts in my direction as I reach maximum sprinting capacity without considering looking back. By the sound of his voice, he's even closer than when I resumed my departure, and running is becoming tiresome. At this rate, escape is merely a desired pleasure. "I have to move faster," I think as the capsule radiates and begins to quickly dissolve into my hand. Out of panic, I violently shake my hand already knowing that it will be ineffective. Satan, still in the same location, clobbers the ground with both fists and roars, "Noooo. You will not defeat me on my own turf. Eden is my kingdom," he ends.

The ground quakes violently again as I finally make it across the lake of fire. I gradually begin to think at this point, "This is hopeless. I'm never going to escape these fiends. So what's the point in running from them," still moving at a fast pace as the container completely dissolves into my left hand. I finally come to the conclusion that I will eventually have to stop running and fight, regardless of this dire situation. In the process of convincing myself, my body begins to slowly glow with the same intensity as the container before it dissipated. The feeling grows to be overwhelming and my body feels weightless. "I am here to help. Witness time, Seer" something speaks deeply.

From the result of the power previously given to me and the capsule now apart of me, something strange occurs. I begin to see random visions develop before my eyes causing me to stumble a bit. However, they're not overcrowding my eyesight because I can still see what I could normally see before. I finally come to a halt, wave my hands in front of my eyes trying to determine what I'm seeing, and then turn around to see if I'll witness the same revelations behind me. The outcome is the same, except the fact that Azrael is now approximately thirty feet away.

"Don't stop now, ignorant fool. I grow fond of the hunt,"Azrael yells and then laughs arrogantly. Seth and Aries grunt wickedly as they jump high over Azrael's head to land on top of me. Completely befuddled by this experience and uncertain of what to do, I close my eyes. Now, more visions heavily engulf my spirit while Satan's voice immediately invades my intellect, "I am God. No matter where you run or where you hide, I'll always be one step ahead," he ends. His image glints inside my head and causes me to frantically reopen my eyes suddenly seeing Azrael jump forward at full speed with his left arm stretched out in front of him in hopes to grab me. Conversely, his right arm is extended out behind him while his hand clinches a fist.

Seth and Aries are now beginning their descent high above my head when three things suddenly happen. First, while images are still rapidly flashing before my eyes, my right eye sparks and decelerates time again to the point where Azrael's left hand is inches away from grabbing my neck, and Aries and Seth are directly above me. Time is now at a snail's pace, but unlike before I'm currently able to move at a normal speed. So, I move to my right to make them eventually collide with each other, and as I do, my body starts to shine even brighter. Second, Satan unexpectedly vanishes from his current location, but not in slow motion. I'm only allowed to witness this happen because the sky was cleared by those pulse waves from the capsule. Needless to say, the clouds are quickly resurfacing. Yet and still, "That's weird. If time is moving so slow, then how could he disappear so fast? On the other hand, since time is creeping, maybe I can really put some distance between us," I think as I turn around to try. This is when the third thing happens.

As I turn around and take my first step with my right foot, Satan emerges one foot in front of me with his left index finger pointing to the sky. Looking directly at me for what seems like an eternity, he tilts his head to the left, shakes his finger back and forth, and grins. "Always one step ahead of you wherever you go, insect. You can't surprise me with the same move twice. Slowing time has no effect on me twice," he declares. Apparently back at full strength, his aura begins to profusely envelop Eden, and sends it into a dark age that's worse than its previous state was. Because of his power replication, he returns time to normal speed causing Azrael, Seth, and Aries to finally slam into each other and fall near my right foot.

Azrael swiftly rises as I return my foot to its original position. While on the ground, Seth and Aries grab my ankles to restrain me from trying to flee again. "You're not going anywhere," Aries speaks. Satan lowers his finger as he laughs. "You will die, suffer, and remain here forever," he exclaims while reaching towards me. With a prompt defensive response from the pod inside of me, it sends out one last pulse wave for a total of seven. This one is undeniably the largest of the seven plus it has an added effect from the star in my right eye.

First, it pushes Satan and his spawns a few feet in the opposite directions from me, and then it begins to change the realm of Eden. In other words, due to these powers strongly working together, Hell is being contained here on Eden in the Sixth Dimension. Neither I nor Satan knows this at the time, but he still gets agitated and exclaims, "You're only delaying the inevitable. You will suffer and die, and I will make you relive it over and over again. Your insignificant god could barely push us ten feet just now, which leaves you hopeless to defeat me. Diiiieee," he screams!!!

Azrael immediately jumps for me again while Satan performs and hurls a hex called the Curse of Anguish and Bereavement towards me.

Seth and Aries both rise and pummel the ground as hard as they can with their left fist at the same time, sending a tremor of earth hastening in my direction. My physical structure and appearance begins to take after that of a ghost, like when I was inside of that barrier, but this time without a protective shield. I quickly fade away at the exact point where Azrael touches the back of my neck with his left index finger, the front edge of the curse nearly taps my lower abdomen region, and the moving ground wave hits my feet all at the same time. Azrael absorbs the full discharge of the curse as it flows through my faded spirit. Unfortunately it doesn't affect immortal as it would a mortal.

Again I'm unseen by Satan and his comrades because I'm unknowingly in the Seventh dimension by what my right eye is showing me. Somehow, I still see them in my left eye along with these random images steady flashing before my eyes, and again Satan is cursing God. The others are looking dumbfounded as he appears to figure out what's happening. "I still feel your presence, fool. The stench of your false father oozes in my nostrils. You will regret the day when I see your face again. And I will see your face again. I will not be restricted or confined to this place because of this...," he lifts up the key that he stole from Michael, "...key. And I will eventually unravel the mysteries of it to destroy all that smell like you," Satan continues to rant.

I personally don't understand what's happening right now, or even how I used any of the powers I previously exhibited. I look around without blinking, but can't recognize anything I see. The moment that I blink, my right eye changes the dimension in my vision but my left eye still sees the Sixth. I'm now unknowingly witnessing the First dimension while seeing the Sixth. "What happened to the other place that I was just in? And how come

Satan can't see me? And why is one eye showing me one thing but the other is different," I ask confusingly?

While I see Satan still bickering about, something says, "You have witnessed the birth of Satan's eternal world of war, chaos, and death. For now, witness his containment within it, and foresee the restoration of the true Eden. There are seven dimensions of time that exist everywhere at once, and each higher level is able to see the lower levels. Though, it is possible to feel the presence of other beings in each of the seven levels when you are in tune to more than one. When he figures this out, he will be able to journey between them all except the 7th. This one cannot be crossed by the likes of evil. For this is the key to the Gates of Himil. All the residents of Himil have been granted access to each gate."

By the response that I'm receiving, I know that I'm speaking with Alpha. However, still confused about what these dimension are, I ask, "Father, I don't understand. What are these dimensions?" I wait for a few seconds hoping to see Alpha when something says, "Come with me, and I will show you." As I'm standing in Hell and the First dimension at the same time, I see an image of the Father which grabs me by the right hand and takes me to the surface of the moon in a metal box. When we arrive, we step out onto the surface while Alpha explains, "All life is my creation, Son. But life is not meant to be all knowing at once. For this I have created seven dimensions that will only flourish if you follow the right paths.

The First Dimension is the preSeed, which has dissolved in you and every creation destined for Eden in the beginning, which is also the end. They are both one in the same, like I am. The beginning is the end, and the end is the beginning. Once you accept this then you will have sight to the Second Dimension, which is the birth of knowledge. This can be easily chosen or forgotten. It's also where Satan began his deceit. However, the Third Dimension is where he walked that path of deceit. This dimension is the path and the way you choose to walk it. It was created for the Seed that chooses to know or forget. Since I did not give the Knowing the choice to walk this path, in other words my angels, then it will be erroneous for them to walk it. Because what is the purpose of choosing if the answer is given? Satan was given the answer and chose the wrong path anyway, and so was punished," Alpha continues by pointing at Eden, which is completely devastated with mayhem and destruction. I look down at Eden and ask, "So If Eden is Hell, then how will the Seed survive? Is it going to be born into a world of Hell," I look at Alpha.

"Remember what I've told you so far, Wajolebe. The Seed will be born into the Third Dimension, not the Sixth. Look at it like this; the First Dimension is the Seed pre-stage. The Second is the Seed accepting the will to choose from me. If the choice is not accepted, then the Seed will not be created until it chooses to be. The Third Dimension is the born Seed choosing the path that it walks. If it chooses righteousness, then it will always walk a straight and correct path. However, if it chooses to walk a path of wickedness, then the path will be in the likes of Satan; forever punishable. This leads me to the Fourth Dimension. This dimension is the sight, which I have given you. The sight allows you to see the goodness or the wickedness in time and life, and the ways to lead the Seed on the right path. The sight can also be used in an evil manner, such as personal gain. However, it will not be given to every Seed, but rather a rare gift. The Fourth Dimension is very important for those who are able or allowed to access it," Alpha continues.

"Finally, the most important Dimension for the Seed is the Fifth Dimension. This one is complicated so pay close attention. First, it can be reached by access points from the Third and Fourth Dimensions like a doorway. The First and Second Dimensions can never access the Fifth because the Seed can only survive in the Third, and with special qualities, access the Fourth. Secondly, when you open the entrance to the Fifth Dimension, you have basically chosen your final destination. This will all be determined by what paths you choose to walk in the Third dimension, or how you prefer to use the Sight in the Fourth Dimension. Remember Wajolebe, when you open the door to the Fifth gate, you will see one of two things. You may see either the path to the Sixth Dimension where Satan dwells, or the Seventh dimension which are the Gates of Himil. The Seventh dimension exists outside of time space and cannot be immorally entered," Alpha pauses and points in two directions. The left hand points towards the Hell on Eden, and the right hand points towards the Kingdom of the Heavens.

I look back at the Father and ask, "So, basically the Seed has to die to see the Fifth dimension?" Alpha touches my forehead and says, "All life that has been created is ordained to change, but once it has become vulnerable it will succumb to Azrael's power. Even then, it does not die, but simply becomes fuel for his essence. Satan uses him for this specific purpose," Alpha pauses as random images of time flashes before my eyes again. I reply, "What are these images, Father? I don't understand." Actually, the images that I see are things that have not happened yet, like the construction of the pyramids, cars, jets, and even something called a Centrical Vortex. Alpha continues, "Use the sight that I've given you, access the Fourth Dimension, learn from it, and become a preacher to the Seeds. Do not preach for say, but edify what you ascertain. Bring them together, and only then will I return to embrace that love. It will be a rough journey, but the pod inside of you carries all the elements of life and knowledge. You also have the power of sight in your right eye to help you on your journey. Do you understand, Wajolebe," Alpha asks?

"I understand, Father. Teach, not preach. Learn, not assume," I respond proudly. Alpha removes his hand from my forehead and says, "All of those images will be random throughout your existence. They will teach you specific things that will help you survive in each era. But for now, let's end this Armageddon on Eden and send it to the Sixth dimension only," the Almighty announces while sweeping both hands back and forth over Eden's figure from the moon. Instantly, Hell is restricted only to the Sixth Dimension on Eden, including Satan and his minions, but Eden is still dark and ruined. "Satan will eventually figure out how to use the key to travel back and forth, and will probably forge it so that his spawns can do the same. Listen closely, Wajolebe. It will seem as though sometimes you'll see something or hear a spirit, but since all life is connected telepathically and each dimension exist in the same time and space, some Seeds will experience ghostly figures of these things. Do not be afraid even of evil, because only then can he harm you. Otherwise, he can only try to influence his surroundings," Alpha stops and looks at me. Before anything is said, I reply, "I understand, and will do my very best to reject his every gesture." Immediately the Almighty smiles, looks back at Eden and says...

Chapter 6: And Let the Light Shine... The Way Through...

"Let there be light to represent day, and the stars and the moon to shine at night" Alpha says while wiping away all of the dirt, ashes, debris, and clouds from Eden. I'm amazed because as the Almighty speaks, the words are being recorded by writing life into the heavens exactly how a manuscript is written. As a matter of fact, Alpha announces, "Let this moment from here on be recorded in harmony forever and ever. I am the Alpha and the Omega, the beginning and the end, the first and the last."

I continue to watch as Eden is being reconstructed into paradise. Everything is being replaced by what was destroyed, and new creations are being introduced at the same time. However the honor of beholding this phenomenal glory doesn't last long because I begin to fade in and out again as I hear the Almighty say, "Take the power that you have acquired and the things you've seen and carry it in your chromosomes. Use the sight to guide you through the times that may seem rough, and the knowledge to educate others. You are wise, Wajolebe, and for this you need not worry. I will be with you at all times. All you have to do is, remember," Alpha's voice echoes out on the word remember. I turn to look at the Almighty one last time as Eden continues to be improved, and then I finally fade completely back inside the metal box. It immediately begins to transport me back to Eden, but something more amazing starts to happen. Time is passing by excessively fast, and millions of years are passing in mere seconds. "I guess time itself is different when you're alongside the Father," I inquisitively say to myself. In actuality, when you stand side by side with the Father, time is considered True Time. In other words, time is motionless. Once you step out of the immediate vicinity, time begins to speed along. I start to think again, "So in theory, if time is this fast when you're close, then the further I move away the slower it should get."

As I travel further away, my theory turns out to be correct. Time is slowing respectively. It kind of reminds me of a planet's gravity. When you're outside of its gravitational pull, you move slowly. However, the closer you get to the planet; gravity pulls you in faster until you cease to move when you reach your destination. In this case, Alpha is the planet and the further you move away from God, the slower things progress. "I just wish that I had some way to record what I'm seeing. I need my note pad to jot down what I see," I state. Unfortunately, my notes haven't been seen since I first left Himil. "All those good notes I took earlier. How will I ever remember everything the Father spoke of? Especially about the seven dimensions. That part seemed to be really important," I pout as a blue orb releases itself from my spirit energy, and slowly floats down to Eden like a feather in the wind. I lose track of it as I eventually land smoothly on verdant soil.

The land is beautiful and time is at a constant pace. "I wonder what would've happened if I stopped at the point where time was moving so fast. Would I have noticed it whizzing by while I was there, or would it have been at a normal pace like it is now," I inquire? Most likely, time would probably appear to be normal wherever you exist, but from the outside looking in it may give off a different impression. I don't waste too much time thinking about it because right now I need to know where I'm located, what era this is, and how I'll fit in. As I start my search, I notice a few things. First, the plant life on Eden is not as enormous as it was when Lucifer created it. Everything is significantly smaller, but basically has the same resemblance. Second, "I'm obviously not in the same era," I say. Third, as I walk a few meters, I observe what looks like tribal markings of different animals on some stones and trees. "This can only mean one thing; other individuals," I deduce. Fourth, I quickly observe myself again to see if I still look the same prehistoric way. When I look at my hands and feet, I see no hair like before. This sight makes me happy, and so I jump for joy. This is when I notice the Fifth and last thing. When I jump, I inadvertently spring a lot higher than I thought I was going to do. "Wow! Super powers? I just thought I would only be able to see things. Amazing," I exclaim with joy! I begin to run, and immediately notice that I can run faster than expected also. However, it's not super fast, but faster than when I was running from Satan and the others.

"I wonder what my face looks like...," I ask out loud and continue, "...if I look like one of them animal drawings on those rocks back there, I'm going to be hot," I deliberately make fun of myself because of how enthused I am. As I continue running through the forest, my mind tells me to look for water of any sort so that I can see a reflection of myself. From what I see up ahead, it looks like I'm about to come up on a lake or something. I eventually run out of the forest and encounter a nice sized creek. I slow my run to a walk and step up to the edge of the rivulet to see my reflection. It's the beginning of the evening, so, "I should see myself pretty good," I say out loud. I kneel down to get a good look at my face and I'm, "Not too shabby. Not too shabby at all. Too bad I look like an eight year old though...Naaaaa! I like being young," I express and continue while standing up, "I wonder if I can jump to the other side," I end.

In reality, a normal athletic person wouldn't get half way across it if they tried to jump. I look around as I'm backing up to make sure that I have enough room for a running start. As I back up a couple of steps, something red catches my eye on the ground underneath a pile of leaves and grass, and postpones my attempt to jump the creek. "What is this," I ask myself? I kneel down to reveal this mystery only to find that it's a red bandana with white dots on it, and as I continue to uncover the full contents of it, I find that it's a sweater underneath to match. "Hmmm. For sure, this isn't the beginning of time on Eden. So, what era am I in then," I curiously question myself as I stand up and strictly analyze the surrounding area? “Maybe there’s something more on the other side of the creek that can help answer my questions,” I propose.

I grab the bandana and sweater with my right hand, back up a few more paces, and sprint forward to jump. The exact moment that my right foot touches the edge of the water, my body slightly shifts so that my head turns to the left. As I lift off the ground, I spot a young girl kneeling by the water a short distance from my current location. She’s holding something oval shaped, and is looking directly at me with a startled look in her eyes. I’m also alarmed to the point where I drop the rags as I escalate over the creek at the water’s edge because I finally detect the orb descending precisely over her head. I look back at her in pre and mid flight out of curiosity until I’m close to landing. When I do land, I turn around once more to observe her response. She doesn’t recognize or sense the orb as it enters her body head first and travels down to her ovaries undetected. Instead, she gasps at the sight of me jumping this far, quickly jumps up from being frightened, and takes off to probably go tell someone that she just saw a ghost that looked like a young boy or girl.

“What just happened,” I ask myself in a muffled voice? I make my retreat into the woods now hoping to find something with a date on it. At first I thought I was somewhere in the early stages of Eden, but with my recent encounter, I may just be in the twentieth century. “Maybe the 1960’s! But how? Did time speed up that much while I was traveling back down to Eden,” I ask myself? I continue to run a few more meters when I hear a horrendous voice say, “The stench of the Almighty fraud. You will not escape me this time,” someone yells out.

Precisely at the point when I hear this, the air around me begins to visibly ripple and the background straight ahead bends back and forth like invisible steam dancing its way to the sky. An enormous amount of energy quickly surges through my body and immediately sends out a pulse wave like before. However, it goes approximately ten feet out in all directions, forcefully returns to me, and swirls ferociously around my body until it forms a spinning ball of energy with me in the middle. As expected by the sound of his voice, Satan's gigantic left arm extends out through the rippling background towards me with the desire to pull me through the dimension into his Hell. However, the energy barrier has already begun to spin me high above his reach while his arm is flailing back and forth trying to grab me. He gets highly upset and quickly pulls his whole body through the wormhole, and looks from left to right like a wild animal until he realizes that I might actually be above him. "There you are," he declares while looking up. He immediately hurls himself up towards me as I begin to spin out of control.

At the moment his left fingertips touch the outside of the energy ball, I disappear without a trail to follow. What I didn't see at the very instant he touched the barrier is a thin stream of dark shadows flowing from his fingertips into my whirling spiritual energy from below. By no means does it harm me, but instead either acts as a tracking device, becomes apart of my DNA, or both. Anyhow, everything happens so abruptly that I never really get a chance to fear the situation. However, I do hear, "Nooooo. I'll get you soon enough, Maggot," Satan cries out after I'm gone.

Somehow I'm being transported through time again, and it seems as though I'm traveling back in the past because everything is going in reverse. The scenery looks weird because plants and trees are growing back into the ground, and birds are flying backwards. Also, everything appears to be getting larger as I continue to travel backwards. "This is cool, but where am I going now. And why do I feel funny," I say as I look at my hands. By the looks of it, I'm growing from a child to a man very slowly because my hands and everything else are increasing in size, but time is speeding backwards. "How is it possible to grow up backwards," I ask myself? Time is speeding along approximately one hundred years every two seconds and only slowing down in defining moments in time. While I try to keep track of what I see, an orb is being released over a little girl's head, at what seems like every century mark or significant moment, exactly like it did the first young girl. Also, as each century skips back, I get a chance to see different wonders of the world and how they're being created. You name it, I'm observing it.

"Wow, this is amazing. I wish everyone could see what I'm seeing right now; all of this knowledge; how to build different types of structures, transport devices, weapons; I know how to do it all," I say astonishingly! Even if I don't get the chance to witness something spectacular, I somehow continue to gain the knowledge of what I miss. While I remain amazed, something strange resembling a diamond exits my body at a rapid pace and vanishes. To be more specific, five more things vacate the premises. They each take the form of skulls made out of different materials, and discharge in various locations at different moments in time as I continue to travel back. No skull lands in the exact same place or time period as another, but each one has a dark flame encasing it.

I reach out to grab a hold of the last one before it completely ejects, but immediately let go of it because of the burn. From the touch of it, the surface feels like a crystallized substance displaying the color black. I would deduce that the material was onyx or some other form of crystal, however I'm not sure. As the last skull ejects, my time traveling episode ends correspondingly. "Those things had the vibe of Satan written all over them, but what were they and where did they go," I ask myself with absolutely no clue of what they are and where they're going.

The skulls were literally Satan's eyes and ears each choosing a specific point in time to reveal them selves as they jettisoned. Each one documented different aspects and angles of everything I saw and learned from the Almighty in this time traveling experience. The actual substances of each were onyx, gold, jade, ruby, sapphire, and diamond. The intelligence gained was preserved within them, and they all contained different information. Since Satan couldn't lay a hand on my spirit, he eventually found another way to try and destroy me.

These skulls hold the key for the time and location of the births of God's special seeds. Basically, Satan will decipher the knowledge from these skulls, reprogram them to include his fraudulent ways, and send them back into the world for people to find with each one containing a different part of him. They will be introduced in various points of time each carbon dated millenniums apart, and shall give birth to his children. However, they will always remain imperishable and journey through every century, respectfully, from their time of location. Once a skull is discovered, from that time until the end, the first woman that touches it will give birth to Satan's spawn, and the child will be enlightened with all the information concealed within that particular skull. When the mother dies, the next woman to find it and touch it will produce the same results. If the child dies then the cycle skips to the next woman's touch. However, if or when all of the skulls are discovered and assembled, then torment will be unleashed from the pits of Hell unless the child from the orb of the Almighty hinders the event. There will only be one child per period from the orb, but there may be more than one from each skull.

Satan plans to employ his spawns with forbidden knowledge to eventually annihilate God's children once and for all. If he can't touch their spirits with his hands, then he will destroy their souls with the hands of his children. And for each one of his children that commit this treason will suffer a mighty curse on their heads by the hand of God. Again, these things I do not know, but I'm sure that I'll be the first to find...

"Now where am I, and what period is this," I ask as I'm drifting back to Eden's soil. I see nothing around me to offer a clue, but I do hear very faint and strange voices either singing or chanting. “That’s odd. Where is that coming from,” I ask myself? The closer I get to land, the louder it becomes. However, I still see nothing. “Maybe it’s my imagination,” I think before I actually come up with a logical explanation for it. “I might just be in a different dimension,” I proclaim. Needless to say, I use my right eye’s dimensional vision for the first time, and I see only God looking back at me. “Did I do something wrong,” I say to myself softly. Alpha smiles at me, and then replies, “No, my son. You did everything right. And now I need for you to rest a while.” I’m surprised that my voice was heard and so I respond, “I’m so glad that you can hear me, but why am I resting, Father?” After a short pause, Alpha replies, “I need for you to make this person see what you see while I continue to work. Place that being into your eyes until I’ve completed my task.”

I look around to see who is surrounding me, but I see nobody. I reply, “Whom are you speaking of, Father? I don’t see anyone. Is it those voices that I hear singing and chanting?” God then points towards me and says, “The individual that reads your journal; the reader of your spiritual encounters. Look outside of your pages, Wajolebe. In the meantime, I will rejuvenate your spiritual energy one last time while you do so. Time may seem to elude you in the upcoming moments, but I will give you the knowledge that is overlooked. You give that person your eyes for now and let them witness these moments so that they will understand. Put them in a dream state so that they can walk in your shoes,” Alpha ends as my journal rematerializes into my right hand. I look at it wondering who’s reading it, but I can’t see anybody. “Am I forgetting to do something or say something? Maybe that’s it. Maybe I should say something...Is anybody out there reading these pages,” I ask very loudly. No one responds.

“I said, is there someone out there reading these pages,” I scream louder as I stare at the journal even harder. At this point something strange begins to happen. The book starts to oddly move like the ripples in water until, "Huh!!! What is...I think I see something," I pronounce while looking at a figure on the opposite end of my journal. The size of the body of who I see is about that of an unborn baby in its third month. I can barely see this figure, so the size may be a miscalculation from the distortion. I'm definitely not for sure if I'm right, but, "Whoever you are, take my sight and witness what God has in store for you. Don't be afraid. Yeah, I'm talking to you, right there. I have to put you into a dream state so that you can see what I've seen and more. God wants me to do this for you right now, but I don't know how long it'll actually be for," I look back at Alpha and continue. Is this the right person? Did I say the right things," I end.

Alpha smiles and replies, "Yes, there's only one person reading your book now. That person is already in a dream state. Hurry and show them what I show you while your spirit is being restored. Things will be different here than out there where the Reader is. Everything will be much slower on the other end; even what you say. So, are you ready," Alpha questions me? I look at you and say, "I hope you're ready for whatever you're about to witness. From what it seems, I have to narrate your dream. I hope you understand everything that I'm supposed to tell you. Blessings," I say to you as I nod my head to God. I keep my focus on your aura as things begin to slow down to normal speed for you, "Oh, by the way, what is your name. My name is WaJohnLeeBe," I say to you, as I finally figure out what Wajolebe stands for. You tell me your name, but somehow I immediately forget it because of how tired I'm becoming.

Anyhow, I say my name again for good measures as time slows to its final stage, "Wa...de...Johnni...e...Lee...Bell...Wow! That's so simple. Wajolebe is my whole name spoken super fast. I guess when time completely slows down; I can here the full pronunciation. Wade Johnnie Lee Bell. That's cool. Anyway, I'm ready, Father," I say as my eyes begin to close uncontrollably. Actually, it feels like God is putting me to sleep while showing me visions of what to say to you. "This is most likely the only way that we can really communicate, so here goes," I say as I begin to recite the visions to you.

Time...what is time? To you, Time is more than likely completely different in God's eyes. For example, if God was to take just a small amount of time to rest, it would probably seem like years to you. A thousand human years may equal one day or less to God. Everything was made to exist by Alpha, and is addressed from a spirits point of view. This is just a piece of the knowledge that God has given me. Are you listening out there? I only ask because I'm getting a vision to describe to you. Here goes...In your dream, you're watching God do all of these remarkable things that I've learned and jotted down as notes in this journal so far, and then you see Lucifer plotting his plan as well. However, you are not seen at all. Imagine watching a movie at a theater with a three dimensional screen. No, not 3D glasses, but the whole screen "Is" the third dimension. Basically, you're inside an actual movie somehow without being noticed or touched. You can't even feel the things in it. You can only see them. Are you imagining yourself in a real live movie under these circumstances? O.k., then let's continue with the dream.

As Lucifer schemes and puts his plan into motion, first you see the equation, "c" plus "C" equals "F", drift past your face. Then, you see three plus three equals six. Finally, you see only a huge six. Remember that c is creating, C is convincing, and F is freedom. Now, imagine that same live action movie theater 3D screen that you're in, and picture these numbers and letters hovering past your face without being apart of the live action movie. They have translucent qualities of a spirit and you can actually feel them whoosh by your face. No one or nothing in the screen, besides yourself, can see or sense the equation. Again, let's continue with the dream.

After you see the six, the dream Flashes like a camera. For a split second in that flash you see Lucifer looking directly at you, face to face, while clutching his fist and frowning. The stare feels as if it penetrates your spirit. You know the feeling that you get when you look up, and somebody's in the room that wasn't there when you looked down; especially when you're in the dark doing something that you don't supposed to be doing? Well multiply that by a number not on the records. THAT FEELING!!!

In a split second you're now on Eden, and you're unseen just as I was. However, this is the beginning of a new Eden, now officially known as Earth, because you see God removing the corruption that Lucifer created and destroyed. The abominations are being replaced with new plants, animals, people, and everything else that you can possibly think of the way that it should be. Not all things of these kinds were removed though. Some remained for purposes only known by God. However, as the days are passing, you see Lucifer again. Somehow, this time, he's different. He has the same six, the one that you saw float by your face earlier; attached to each separate part of his spiritual body in the form of permanent numbers and symbols written in a forbidden language. To be more exact, there's one six on his left and right leg, the front and back of his neck, his forehead, his right and left arm, his chest, and one on his back. He's watching everything that God's doing with an unexplainable hate. As the sixth day ends and God plans the seventh day for rest, you see Lucifer corrupting everything that God has just recreated, out of spite. Then God speaks, "Lucifer, in spite of you and your sadistic ways, you shall be cursed on this day forever. On the day after I rest, I shall create another place where your Pure Evil spirit will not be allowed access."

As planned, God rests on the seventh day. After you witness the confrontation between God and Satan, you see a second six hover by your face. Only this time it finds its' way over to Satan and positions itself next to the first six on each separate part of his spiritual body. This is officially the second six, and it signifies the God day that Satan was cursed on.

Next in your dream, you see God resting and planning everything that will take place on the next day. Remember that equation you saw float by before; well now you see one that God has formulated. "F" plus "D" minus "C" equals "G". Then it eventually turns into six plus four minus three equals seven. Finally, you see just a huge seven. All of a sudden, you hear God's voice speaking to you and only you. "Faith plus determination minus the corruption will equal godliness. This is my plan to suppress Lucifer's evil actions." Immediately you see this equation coming towards you, growing with intensity and speed, and then slowly passing through your body. Flash; you know...the whole camera thing again. This time you see God pointing at you, and its' making you feel the best you've ever felt in your life. Imagine the feeling, if you can, of a seriously supercharged electric current or static shock flowing through your body unexpectedly except without the pain. Multiply that jolt by a number not on the records, and then add that to the best feeling you've ever had in your life. Just like that, only you see it coming and you don't want to move. Some will say that this is God's spirit flowing through you; the Holy Spirit.

In a split second again, you're back on Eden. This time you're watching God place a garden off to the side with trees, animals, and people in it. It's identical to what's outside of the garden before it was corrupted by Lucifer, except on a smaller scale. While God is situating everything, you turn to observe Lucifer in the distance pacing, trying to figure out a way to defy the Father's spoken word again. To him, it always has to be some type of loophole to unearth. So, he starts mumbling to himself until he finally comes to a conclusion on how to enter the garden. He found a loophole. To enter the garden, he needs to hide his spirit's aura. Once inside, he can reveal himself and instantly corrupt everything that he deems necessary. He somehow needs to use a body to carry his spirit inside undetected, and then do his dirty work from there. What I'm describing is about to become the first possession in the history of life. A person will most likely be discovered in particular because the Will, or mind, is too easy to corrupt. However, animals have a different Will.

They have natural instincts which are hard to corrupt, but just as easy to possess. The difference between humans and animals is; we have instincts that we choose to use, but on the contrary, animals are bound for eternity to live by their instincts. In other words, they do what they have to do and we choose to do what we please. Flash; except the only difference is, this time the flash remains constant like white sunlight). Lucifer begins to walk towards you in a hasty manner as if he has discovered you unveiling his plans. Eden and everything else disappears, and again it's just you and him looking directly at each other six inches apart. You begin thinking, "Where am I suppose to go? There's nowhere to run to, and even if there was, my legs won't allow me to move." Imagine that you're getting caught doing something wrong again, but now you're getting reprimanded for it in the worst conceivable way. And to top it off, you can't escape. Multiply that by another number not on the records, then add that to the fact that you're paralyzed. This is what you're experiencing at the moment.

In a split second for the last time, Eden reappears and you're above it looking down at the ground where you were just standing a minute ago. It feels as if you're standing on a sturdy foundation, but there's only air and clouds. Can you feel that platform? Okay, as I was saying, you're now looking down at the spot where you ascended from, and you see a snake with legs. Then you look in the direction in which Satan is coming from, and you see that he's trying to possess every animal that he touches. He continues to reject all of them as he passes by. It seems as though they are being abandoned because they're not providing enough protection from his spirit being exposed.

Anyhow, at the same time that he's frantically searching, God completes Eve as you descend into the garden. On your way down, you catch a glimpse of Satan finally finding the snake as a suitable host. Of course your instincts are kicking in right now, so you try to warn God from a distance by waving your hands and screaming. At this moment, you're thinking that you can participate in the dream because it seems so real. However, this is not the case. Remember, you're unable to be seen or touched. You're only here to witness what I relay from God. Don't loose sight of this because it may come back to bite you later. Trust me, I previously found out the hard way when I was that hairy creature.

Nevertheless, you finally touch down in the garden. The first thing that you notice is that you can't see what's transpiring outside the garden. What your eyes are portraying right now looks like a double sided mirror showing you only the elements of Earth on the opposite side of it. For example, the mountains, trees, sky, ground, and water. However, no humans or animals are visible by your eyes. Everyone on the outside has the same visuals as you. Basically both sides are invisible to each other with the exception of some animals.

Unexpectedly, your dream rewinds to the part where God tells Lucifer, "...pure evil spirit will not be allowed access...," then it immediately fast forwards to a part of your dream that you didn't get a chance to observe happen. This part shows you what Satan has uncovered about the garden. He knows that his access is denied spiritually, but he's not for sure if it'll be hidden from his sight as well. This is where the idea for possession plays a major role, and also how it may pave his way into the garden. You overhear

Lucifer say, "Yeesss. An innocent eye is the key. I have figured you out again, Idiot. And I shall be there to destroy your vision," he ends.

After Satan's speech, you instantly transport back to the present in your dream, only to find that you've missed a lot since you were gone. Maybe not too much, but it's enough to let you know that God has placed another curse on Satan for entering the garden and deceiving Eve with the first skull that entered the third dimension; the Onyx skull. It was buried under the Tree of Knowledge of Good and Evil, and thus made the tree corrupt to eat from. The skull programs Eve's DNA with false knowledge, and permits her to give birth to an evil spawn; Cane. As a result, she has to procreate with Adam, which sequentially curses them both. A curse is also placed upon the head of the serpent as a result of Satan's previous curse of damnation for eternity on the sixth day, and for allowing him access into the garden. Satan and the snake will be linked symbolically until the end of time. You begin to hear God speak the curse, "For associating yourself with this evil spirit, you have defied my orders. And for such misdeeds, you will wear his mark forever." This is where the third six floats by your head and attaches itself next to the other two sixes on Satan's body as God continues, "And you will crawl on your belly as an apology to me each day for as long as you exist. Of this day, everyone will identify your mark as his. You will be forever linked to his evil," God ends as one six is placed in each eye of the snake. The curses that are issued by the Almighty are never harmful, but are only mere consequences that are brought upon the doer by the doer for all creations to witness.

The Father is telling me right now that this part of your dream may get a little scary because Satan is not very happy at the moment, and will most likely retaliate. Remember those terrible feelings that I asked you to imagine earlier? Well, how I'm about to describe what you feel now, is off the scale of thinking. You'll have to feel exactly what I describe next, word for word. Let your imagination separate itself from any physical barriers that you may have. Here goes!

After God places the six in the eyes of the snake, there's a moment of silence. Adam and Eve disappear, the garden vanishes, and finally everything else just fades away. It's only you, God, and Satan in this eccentric void. There's no light, dark, time, or any form of life for this matter. Nothing exists. It's just you three occupying the same space at the same time, which is physically impossible to the human mind. This means you're personally allowed to feel all, but somehow at the same time, you seem to be further away from them than they are to each other. It's like everyone just is with nothing else involved. If you're having a hard time breaking the barriers of physics, just picture God and Satan within talking distance of each other, and you're at a safe distance watching them unnoticed. Oh, by the way, God says to stop drifting in thought sometimes and hear only what I'm suppose to convey to you at this moment.

Now to continue your dream; you overhear God say to Satan, "I have shown you mercy because I am a forbearing father. I created you for a reason, my son. You have a purpose like all creations, which is to fulfill what is. Time and again you have journeyed beyond the limits in which I've authorized for you, and have been punished for each sin that you've committed. Likewise, you will be punished thereafter. So heed my warning, Satan. There will be Seers in time to restrain your wickedness and refute your name. These prophets will be my sons spiritually and physically, and will be known as my Sons of Man. By name they will arise to send you back to the depths from which your evil spirit resides."

At this moment, you feel the urge to say something like, "Yeah! That's right! Put him in his place, and let him know who the boss is too." However, it's pointless because you're unseen, unheard, and basically not a factor in the outcome of events in this entire dream. What better way to be a witness, right? At this exact point in your dream, is when you accept these facts and finally decide to observe it burden free. Satan replies, "I don't need your mercy, Imposter," he snickers and continues. "And I don't answer to no one except me. I create my own fate like your mortals, and that's why I'm able to journey beyond your pathetic limits. And what makes you think that I'm the least bit concerned about your ineffective curses. They haven't curved my appetite to overthrow your rule so far, and they never will, Liar," Satan says heartlessly as he turns his back towards the Almighty, pauses, and then begins to speak again. "Oh, and as for your prophets restraining me...," he says while looking over his left shoulder irately, "...I will bring death to each and every one of them time and again. And that's including..."

From point "A", where Lucifer is standing in front of God, to point "B" located precisely where point "A" is; which immediately seems like ten miles from point "A"; which is where you're standing; Satan appears in no seconds flat looking you directly in the eyes again like he did previously. Point "A, where God is located, is now literally ten miles from point "B". A half of a second passes and you're not afraid since you know for a fact that you're invisible to the events in the dream, but you're still a little uncomfortable because of what the situation looks like. This is including the facts of how fast he appeared in front of you and the look you're receiving from him right now. Another half of a second passes and you're now thinking about how he knew to appear two inches away from the spot that you're standing in, and you're becoming more nervous.

So as the next second passes, you make sure that you're unseen by gently sliding to the right because it may be possible that he feels your presence instead of actually seeing you. Another half of a second passes and you begin to regain your confidence that you are undetectable because he's still standing motionless in the same spot that you're shifting from. Another half of a second passes and his eyes still don't follow you. Your nerves begin to calm, and you breathe a sigh of relief as another second passes. However, you don't take your eyes off of him just yet. You want to give it a couple more seconds to be absolutely convinced. For reassurance and valor, as the fifth second passes, you feel the need to know that God is still at point "A". You slowly cut your eyes in that direction during the start of the sixth second. At this point you feel your heart rise to your throat and the sensation of fear kindling throughout your body because as you move your eyes, you think that you're seeing Satan move his towards your direction.

Within this same second, you also think you see his eyebrows slant angrily. This is when the seventh and final second passes; the point where your heart skips a beat and the kindling of fear is now an immense flame. Satan's head slowly tilts towards you with his eyes focused on yours, and his top lip and eyebrows lifted. You instantly redirect your attention to him realizing in the process that he can see you. An unspeakable feeling surges through your veins at this point as Satan completes his sentence from seven seconds ago that you thought was meant for God, "...you," he ends while grabbing you by the throat with his left hand at, what seems like, light speed.

You're in shock, and you can't move a muscle as he begins to speak again, "You will suffer by my hand as one of the so called chosen, and you shall die as one of the Sons of Man. No one opposes my name," Satan speaks heavily as he lifts you up by your throat. Out of the blue you hear an earsplitting noise worse than the loudest recorded thunderstorm, eruption, or explosion combined. It's Satan roaring, without even opening his mouth, as he lifts you above his head. You begin kicking and beating on his left arm, trying to remove his hand from your neck as the roar continues to grow louder.

It's useless. His grip is too tight. The more you struggle, the more it seems as if he grows stronger. So eventually, you refuse to resist any longer. This idea seems to be the wisest thing to do at the moment because by not letting him feed on your struggles, will probably result in him thinking that you're dead and leaving you alone. Satan looks over his left shoulder towards the Almighty and speaks as the noise intensifies, "Seer? You call this a Seer. Huh," he looks back and you and continues! "You're weak. You carelessly believe that I will become powerless if I'm ignored and discarded. Reminds you of someone, Father," Satan asks God in a taunting manner? At the same time, he cocks back his right hand forcefully and says to you, "Impudent fool. I can only get stronger," he laughs as the noise peaks. While laughing, he jams his right hand into the center of your torso with an unheard of force. However, no physical damage is dealt to your body, just a ton of pain. You immediately get cold and hot simultaneously, and your body begins to shake vigorously and continuously from the force of his fist impacting your chest. You can slowly feel his evilness creeping into your mind trying to take your spirit and soul.

You turn your head towards God with hopes of support, but you receive none. Instead, the image of the Almighty slowly fades on the horizon. At this point you start to believe that God has no love for you because he's allowing one of his own to go through this. You've done nothing wrong, and so begin to feel alone and vulnerable; like you want to call it quits. However, you're not going out without a fight. So you break out of your non resisting mode and begin to struggle a little harder than before; kicking, biting, scratching, swinging, and punching. You're doing it all but nothing changes.

Satan continues to laugh as the cold and hot feelings grow more severe. With no mercy, he digs deeper by forcing his whole spirit inside of your body. You're being possessed while your body is still hoisted in mid air by your neck. At the moment, you don't know what to do, so you begin to fight even harder. However, physically fighting back isn't working and you're almost out of options until you actually figure out what he's really doing to you. He's not trying to take your spirit and soul, but only trying to kill your spirit to control your soul. That's why he reached for your heart and not your mind.

You gradually begin to regain your strength and confidence back, which in turn makes you want to give Satan a piece of your mind. So, repeat after me. You have to say this part to get rid of him, "You know that you can't control the Will if there's a strong presence of spirit. So you must find a way to weaken the spirit by damaging the body hoping to confuse the Will. Then you destroy the spirit to control the mind and body. And if I'm not mistaken...," you strangely start to yell in a deep demonic voice that Satan makes you speak in, and continue, "...this is my spirit, my Will, and my body along with everything else that comes with the package," you continue while noticing the light of the Almighty on the horizon becoming stronger. Satan gradually begins to lose control over you, and you start to speak in a more controlled voice, "You're inside of my body, Satan. This means that I'm the landlord and you're the tenant. And you're late with the rent. Now get out," you demand. You feel a sudden rush of anger, and you immediately drop out of the air onto your side. The impact of the landing stuns you for at least thirty seconds.

You slowly open your eyes looking directly towards the Almighty's last position, expecting to see a smile. Instead, you see nothing again. However, this time you feel a wondrous feeling, as if you've just defeated the most challenging obstacle known to man, or yourself. This feeling is the work of the Almighty inside of you. At last, you finally become fully conscious to the sound of Alpha's voice saying, "Satan's evil presence was cast out. You are strong mentally, physically, and spiritually, and you have the power to help others become strong in the likeness of yourself.

Faith alone will never defeat Satan. You also have to know your adversary and what he's capable of, to know the faith that will defeat him. Ignorance of him will end in your bereavement. Your faith in me will always be exposed, but my faith in you reigns supreme and can never be tainted.

You've now earned the right to become a renowned preacher, but instead I want you teach. Teach the people that not only should they have faith in me, but that I faith in them as well. When all becomes the same, then shall I return," Alpha points towards Eden, showing you how everyone should come together and love one another the same. "However, beware of the deceitful one. He will always be after you and everyone else walking in my glory. Rebuke his name, and you shall be rewarded," Alpha concludes. Slowly but surely, the light of Alpha fades into the distance and dissipates.

You eventually recover an adequate amount of physical strength to roll on your back and think about everything that just happened. And you now have questions running through your mind constantly like, "Am I really a renowned preacher? What did God mean by teaching? Isn't preaching and teaching the same thing? Is faith vulnerable?" Of course there are many other questions flowing through your head, but you're not letting them get to you because it's only Satan working his magic again. So you rebuke his name as the father had spoken. Even though he's not inside of you anymore, you've still been contaminated by his touch which may eventually lead to deception. He will always try to influence you to make bad decisions, which will give him the chance to re-enter your body. However, you will not allow it to happen again according to your spirit. At this point you slowly raise your left hand to rub your face as if you just woke up, and as you begin, you hear Alpha calling out, "Wajolebe, wake up. Your time has come."

As your figure quickly fades from my sight to the sound of God's voice, I awake simultaneously saying, "It was nice talking to you, whoever you were." When I come to, I see God pointing to Earth while saying, "You have to go now. Take your spirit to Earth to develop. Teach the others what I have taught you in your journal," God pauses. I notice that the journal has disappeared again and ask, "What happened to my book, Father? It disappeared on me again. How can I remember everything that you've taught me to edify if I don't have my notes," I end? God replies, "The journal is your book of life. It will always remain in spirit, and can never be lost," Alpha pauses again. This particular response from God left me with one last question, "Who was I just talking to then, Father?" The Almighty turns to me and answers, "When the Will to choose is accepted, then your spirit will encode the book of life to match your soul. Only then will you know that answer and understand your question. Are you ready to accept the will to choose from me, Wajolebe," the Almighty asks? I quickly come to a conclusion about where I am and what's actually happening right now when I'm asked this.

So, I begin thinking to myself, "If I'm correct, this is what the Father spoke of previously about the dimensions. A spirit will remain in the First Dimension until the Will to choose is accepted. Then a seed will be created and entered into the Second Dimension until it's born. The Second Dimension is where a spirit is taught all knowledge," I pause as another notion hits me at the same time. "Wait a minute. Am I not born then," I silently question myself? Out of the blue, I start to remember something else about the dimensions. "If the choice is not accepted, then the Seed will not be created until it chooses to be. The Third Dimension is the born Seed choosing the path that it walks," the exact words from Alpha recaps in my head.

I still don't respond to the Father's question just yet because, over time, I came to accept the fact that Satan is a great impressionist. He could most definitely be trying to con me into believing that he's God in hopes to falsify my existence. But In the middle of all of this, I'm suddenly interrupted by those weird sounds of people singing and chanting again. As I begin to see indistinct figures hovering a little ways in front of me, everything else starts fading to black except those figures. However, I don't get an evil feeling of any kind. I'm still thinking about the question and I want to answer it, but I'm not for sure if Satan is playing a trick on me.

Then again, as I continue to think about it, he wasn't there when God explained the dimensions to me. So, without prolonging the Father's question anymore, I finally say, "No, I do not accept the Will to choose from you, Father," I announce with dignity. Alpha's voice speaks, "Wise choice, Wajolebe. You still have much to learn. I have given you a choice, and you made it without my interference. And this will always be so. Remember this one important thing; you will always uncover Satan's trickery if there is any confusion about who I am or what I've done. This you will figure out because of his interference. And there will always be confusion with his interferences. Since you have made a choice, your home will become the Second Dimension until you are ready to be born. In addition, you have the sight to journey through the other dimensions to gain more knowledge, worry free. Time will pass at an immeasurable speed in some instances, but the knowledge of it all will catch up with you eventually and reimburse your memory; even if you don't initially know it. This is my gift to you. Now go, and work my wonders in spirit until you're ready to accept the will to choose," Alpha's voice echoes out.

Immediately, everything comes back to light and I'm back on Earth. The ghostly figures are no longer indistinct, and the voices are no longer mysterious. I see complete figures of a group of seven people straight ahead chanting, "Please Divine one, ease her pain, and comfort her through this childbirth. She has come to us to enquire of you." When I hear "childbirth", I curiously make my way over towards the group to see who they're speaking of. Behind them is a woman laying in the bed asleep. I look around to analyze my surroundings, and I may just be in a very small holy shelter of some sort. To my surprise, one man in the group acknowledges my presence by looking directly into my eyes. I immediately increase my guard level, but he seems harmless because he makes everyone else bow as if I was God; even though, to my knowledge, they can't see me. In return, I bow to prove that I'm not. The one gentleman quickly rises up, rushes towards me, and stops my gesture by helping me back up and saying, "No, no, no. You do not bow to us, we bow to you." I'm completely stunned by the fact that he can actually touch me.

So, I ask, "How are you able to see and touch me, and who are you," I ask? He bows again while replying, "We are oracles, and we've been tasked to enquire about young lady Rebecca's expectancy. Can you bring peace to her pregnancy," he ends? By what he said, I'm almost certain that I know what era I'm in, and I say to myself, "Rebecca. I don't think that I've ever heard this name before. Or have I?" Exactly as promised by the Almighty, time hits me like a blinding flash of light and things become clear. "Rebecca. Esau. Jacob," I say to myself inexplicably. In that quick flash of light, I also receive visions of a blue orb finding its way into Eve, and Abel being the outcome of it. I'm even more stunned when I see Cane, born from the Onyx skull, killing his twin brother. The flash ends, and by impulse reaction, I speak out loud, "I've traveled back this far." The oracle wastes no time in commenting, "Esau and Jacob. We know of no Esau and Jacob. Who do you speak of, my Lord?"

I heave a sigh and reply, "I am not God, Oracle. However, the same Lord that you serve is also my Lord. As for Esau and Jacob, they will be the identical offspring's born from young lady

Rebecca. May I ask you a question though," I inquire? The oracle shakes his head in accordance. I continue, "How come you're the only who's able to see me." He turns his head as he stretches his hand out towards the others, and says, "We all can see and hear you, and we all know that you descended from the heavens. Nonetheless, please forgive us for mistaking your worth." I immediately look towards the others as they lift their heads to look at me. I reply, "But I thought...never mind. Why do you assume that I came from heaven," I ask? He then turns and points towards Rebecca as he speaks, "About five moons ago, Lady Rebecca came to us and spoke of a dream that she experienced three and half moons prior. In that dream, she was kneeling at the river's edge and heard a noise whisper above her head. She decided to look up as something that resembled a human's face hit her over the head and knocked her unconscious without the opportunity to avoid it. At the exact same time, she saw a blue sphere enter her body through her eyes while they were closing as she begins to fall from the impact of the human face. When she finally came to in the dream, there was a man with a blue aura surrounding him, standing over her and making her feel like she would soon be apart of something special. She didn't know where he came from, but he delivered peace to her fighting womb," he pauses as he looks back at me and continues, "And if you don't mind me saying; we thought that you were the Almighty father because as you can see, Lady Rebecca is still asleep and you have that very unique blue essence around you," he ends.

I turn to look at Rebecca as I say to him, "Eight and a half moons most likely means about nine months ago. But a blue orb, you say? That's very good news! Wait a minute; did you say a human's face," I ask as I suddenly become bothered? The oracle shakes his head in agreement as I continue, "That's not good. Did you check her head for a mark of any sort?" He looks confused by my agitation and replies, "What type of mark, and why would I be looking for it?" As I start to jog over, I respond, "Any type of mark, because then that would mean her dream was real. And if her dream was real, then that human's face is really a skull somewhere nearby. And if the skull is nearby, then we have to either find it and destroy it, or find it and restrain it so that it will never be found if it can't be destroyed," I end as I reach her and begin searching.

"So, the human's face is a bad omen," he asks? I give him a look that means yes, and reply, "Anything created by the hands of Satan is never good. He just makes it seem as such," I express as I actually find a permanent mark on her forehead under her tresses. The Oracle has no clue of what I'm referring to or what to ask, so he just stands quiet. During this time, Rebecca immediately wakes up from the physical contact and says blissfully, "My prayers have been answered, and..." Without haste, I rudely interrupt and respond, "Not yet they haven't, Lady Rebecca. I need to find out if you have something in your possession or know of it. Did you find a crystal-like skull about eight and half months ago," I ask? She gives me the look of a confused unintelligent person, and asks, "What is mon...mont." I promptly interrupt her failed pronunciation and continue, "I'm sorry; eight and a half moons ago?"

She understands my question and answers promptly, "Yes. Yes. I placed it in that haystack beside the manger. Ooohh!!," she moans as she sits up from the pain of the two brothers fighting inside of her, while grabbing her stomach. I quickly rush over to find the skull to discard of it. As I fumble through the haystack I finally come upon it. The surface of it looks to be made of Gold and not of onyx like the visions I recently saw, but some of the hay surrounding is black. I reach out to grab it with my right hand, but my hand becomes transparent and misses the target. I try again, and the same thing happens. "Why can't I touch this thing," I ask out loud in frustration?

Immediately I'm hit with another flash of light that lasts less than a second. However, in that flash I hear a very familiar voice say, "Let's confuse them so that they won't understand each other." That same voice then says "...sacrifice your son to me to prove..." Another flash hits me, and in that flash I see Satan's face accompanied with a sharp scream. After this, more and more flashes strike me with a voice repeating over and over again, "I am a jealous God. Put no other God before me." As the voice keeps reiterating, I see flashes of Satan's face each time it does. The visions become puzzling, and so I begin to shake my head from left to right violently with my hands on it. The Oracle and Rebecca asks simultaneously, "Are you alright?" I become very confused because I now have questions inside of my head about these sudden vision, like, "Why would God try to confuse what already is, and then become jealous of it? Why? It doesn't make sense." At this moment, another flash strikes me with a voice that says, "And there will always be confusion with his interference."

The flashes end and I immediately reply to the Oracle and Rebecca's previous question, "Yes, but you won't be, Rebecca." She looks at the Oracle and then back at me while saying, "What do you mean? Is there something wrong?" I remove my hands from my head as I gaze at the golden skull and say, "Yes, there is something wrong. This skull has placed a curse on one of your sons to be. The blue sphere that you dreamed is just as real as this skull, and it comes directly from the Almighty. The son that will be born from it will be God like, but unfortunately will be killed by the evil son of the skull," I try to continue, but I'm cut short by Lady Rebecca. "How do you know this for sure," she asks with much concern. I reply, "I had many visions just now, but the last one showed me this. However, I didn't receive an answer on how to resolve the problem for you, or prevent it from happening. This may be because the Lord wants you to make your own decision on how to fix it," I say as I slightly shrug my shoulders.

Rebecca, not knowing anything about what's actually happening right now, asks, "Well, what do you recommend, honest man?" Before I respond, the Oracle steps up and comments, "If you are from the Almighty, then so will be your answer." I look at Rebecca and say, "I may have descended from God, as does everything in existence. However, I am separate and therefore not perfect. My answer will not meet your expectations, Lady Rebecca." Rebecca smiles at me and replies, "But don't you see, Good Sir; it just did." I reply with a dumbfounded look on my face, "Huh?"

The Oracle adds on to Rebecca's statement by humbly saying, "Separate. Separate is the answer. With your honest response came the perfect answer. Separate," he ends. Rebecca continues, "I will find a way to separate my sons when the time comes to do so. They will grow as brothers and will not be separated unless I detect the smallest hint of evilness in one of them. Until that time, they will always remain by my side. Thank you...Uuhhh...who may I refer to you as, sir," she asks? The moment I open my mouth to answer, I begin to fade away. I look at both of my hands blinking in and out, and I hear a very concerned Rebecca say, "No, don't go. We have yet to acquire a name from you, good sir." As I completely fade away, I reply, "Wajolebe. My name is Wajolebe."

The Oracle turns to Rebecca and says, "God is with you, Wajolebe. As is with you too, Rebecca," he ends. Rebecca looks towards the golden skull and ask, "How must we destroy this evil thing, Oracle?" He turns towards it and says, "If Wajolebe couldn't pick it up, then maybe it wasn't meant for a pure soul to touch it. This may also indicate that it's indestructible. If this is true, then you must bury it deep, deep in the ground where no man will ever think to look," he ends as time eventually begins to fast forward again for me.

"I wonder what new adventure approaches," I say to myself. I'm actually hoping that I end up back at that creek where I saw that little girl, but pretty much I believe that I won't. Honestly, I don't know why I keep thinking about her. Meanwhile, Satan is encoding and preparing the other skulls for their entrance into the world at the exact points in time where they previously ejected from my spirit. Again, I have no clue of his actions. However, I've figured out what the skulls are capable of. They are capable of assisting a woman in giving birth to an evil child. Two things led me to this theory. First, Rebecca is having an evil son of two, according to her dream and my visions. Secondly, Cain was born from the skull and killed his twin brother Abel. "Is this a sign that this will happen to me when I finally decide to say yes to God," I ask myself? Time continues to fast forward decades at a time. I'm seeing history being made across the world in different locations and times, and I say out loud, "Amazing. Have these things already happened, or am I seeing the future," I ask because I've seen some of these visions when I traveled back the first time. "Maybe they'll be important later," I say to myself.

I have tons of questions, especially about those visions I received when I was with the Oracle and Rebecca, but I'm not going to ask them because I believe that I will receive an answer in due time. There's on thing that I've learned on this journey of mines so far; time just is. It's the resonance of God, and so is the beginning and the end. God has set forth a current that ripples as it flows throughout our space, and those ripples are made for our utilization. However the current stays the same and can never be changed. The end has been set, but we determine how to employ those ripples as they are carried through time. You can choose to struggle and drown as you reach the end, or build a boat to smooth your voyage. I choose to build a boat and ride the current all the way to the end. "Yeah! That's it! I finally get it now. There's nothing that can change the end because it's already written. The choices that we make only determine how fast or slow we arrive. However, what's at the end," I ask out loud? Time begins to slow down as if it overheard my comments. Out of nowhere comes another voice that may just be Alpha's voice replying, "That's the miraculous question."

I start to look around to locate the voice as time slows down again, drastically. I can't locate it, so I reply, "How will I know when I'm ready to find out. How will I prepare myself to know," I ask? Silence falls upon me for a short second, and then the voice responds, "All you have to do is wake up. The answers are right in front of you. Just wake up." I continue to look around for the voice as time halts and I finally touch ground again. As I look around, I notice that this place looks familiar. "This looks like the same time period where I saw that little girl. Have I returned here again," I ask silently? Anxiously, I begin to run straight ahead like before.

While running, I think to myself, "If this is the same timeframe, then I should see animal drawings over there...," I look towards the direction on my right and continue, "...there it is. Can it be the same ones...," I run fast like before hoping to see a creek up ahead, "...If there's a creek up ahead then it's definitely the same place," I end. As the trees begin to clear, I finally come upon the creek, but, "Where's the little girl," I ask out loud. I unsuccessfully scan the area with my eyes becoming more and more disappointed, until I hear leaves slowly crunching in the distance. I immediately run towards the spot where I saw her kneeling down the last time, but nothing. However, to my surprise, something terrifying haunts my vision at the edge of the creek. "What...it can't be," I say slowly kneeling down to get a closer view. The moment that I identify the oval shaped diamond object on the bank, I hear laughter and a loud voice screaming to someone in the distance.

"Karolyn, don't you go out there messing 'round on that creek now or I'mma tell Ma when she get home. You hear me," a girl screams. As I turn around, I see the same little girl skipping towards me in the distance singing, "Ring around the Rosie, pocket full of Posies...ashes, ashes, we all fall down," Karolyn quickly squats down and slowly gets back up from the song. In this short second, I get a flash of the last time I saw her, and that oval object that she had in her hand, "No. I got to stop her. I can't let her touch it, if it is what I think it is," I say frantically. I turn around towards the object to try to pick it up and throw it, but, "I knew it. I can't touch. That means it is one of the skulls, but why is it so much smaller than the other one. And how did it get here before me, when they actually came out of me after I left this place," I begin to quickly ponder as Karolyn gets closer and closer.

She spares me some time by stopping to admire something that catches her attention on the ground, when I suddenly get another flash. In this one I see myself picking up that red sweater from before, and then the flash ends. "I have a plan," I think to myself. I waste no time in running towards the location where I found it the last time, while looking back at Karolyn hoping that she continues to play with whatever it is she's appreciating right now. As I come up on the location, I say enthusiastically, "There it is...," I pick up the red bandana with white dots, and continue, "...and there's the sweater too," I end as I pick that up too. They are both in the same location that I previously found them in.

On the way back I begin wrapping the bandana around my right hand as Karolyn begins skipping again. However, she stops once more to admire something on the ground, as I reach the location of the skull. With the bandana completely wrapped around my hand, I grab at the skull hoping that I can now pick it up and toss it somewhere, and, "Yeeesss. It works," I say. At the same time I quickly undo the bandana to encase the skull while tying the edges in a knot. The skull begins to corrupt the bandana by turning it pitch black from the bottom working its way to my fingertips. Eventually, I won't be able to touch the bandana if I keep holding it right now, but, "I need to toss it where I know she won't go." I look around for a spot as the blackness creeps up the bandana, when, "I got it. I'm supposed to jump over the creek, and she's supposed to see me and run home terrified. So, I have no choice but to toss it in an area that she will be afraid to go," I say as I toss it in the direction that I'm supposed to jump from, aiming for the middle of the creek. "I just hope I show up," I say to myself.

Chances are, even if I don't show up, she won't find the skull because of where it lands in the creek. Unfortunately, she hears the splash and immediately takes her attention off of what she's doing, and skips towards the water where the splash originates. I think to myself, "Aaww man; what should I do now. She's going to follow that noise. Hold up...," I say out loud and continue, "...the sweater, but I can't let her see me, because then she'll really freak out and run the opposite way."

First, I pick up a rock. Next, I toss the sweater into the air towards her direction to draw her attention away from the noise. Then I immediately jump in the opposite direction of my previous self's location, and toss the rock into the water close to wear the sweater should land. As I land in a secure area towards the trees close by Karolyn, the new splash draws her attention to its location. She sees the sweater falling, and starts to skip towards it while saying, "Ooohh, a shirt...," she continues with a song for the sweater, "...It all falls down." I carefully watch in the distance making sure she doesn't go towards my previous location's first appearance. "I really hope I show up," I say silently. That same voice I heard previously says again, "Wake up, and you will see what the end is like." I continue to watch as I finally see myself jumping over the creek. At this point, Karolyn is holding the red sweater in her hand, instead of the diamond skull, while watching my other self jump over the creek. The blue orb descends into her body just the same as before, and then she takes off running. I remain hidden thinking to myself, "I didn't actually believe that I would show up because I'm already here. So how am I able to be in two places at the same time? Was I here all along? Is this where I suppose to be?"

That same voice returns and says, "All you have to do is wake up. Close your eyes, concentrate, and wake up." I'm very confused at this point because God never actually tells me the answers to my own questions, or even how to solve my own problems when I'm personally involved.

More puzzled, I inadvertently stand up and begin walking in the same direction that Karolyn is running in, with my right hand rubbing back and forth on my chin contemplating, "Maybe this is God trying to enlighten me by showing me the way. But even if it is the Almighty, I still have to make my own choice regardless...," I pause and then continue to myself, "...I know what I'll do! I'll follow Karolyn...," I look up to see Karolyn far off bypassing an outhouse, and then I continue,"...and if I detect the smallest hint of interference, then this time I'll fight back."

I pick up the pace to catch up with Karolyn, but it begins to seem like I'm not closing the distance at all. I initially don't think anything weird of it, until I start moving at top speed and Karolyn is still gaining distance. "How is this possible? I'm running full speed, but I'm virtually stationary," I think to myself. I get this odd feeling to look back, but I ignore it and continue to push forward as hard as I can. Suddenly the ground directly below me begins to move the opposite way, just as fast as I move onward. It feels like I'm on some type of moving mat, but when I look down, nothing's moving. "What," I proclaim! Again, my instincts urge me to look over my shoulder, but I deny it once more. I'm more focused on catching up to Karolyn, even though it seems impossible.

"Close your eyes and wake up before it's too late," the voice says again behind me. Originally, I was avoiding the need to look back, but when I hear the voice behind me, instinctively I do. The moment I turn around, I see this thing emerging from the middle of the creek where I tossed the diamond skull. It wasn't Satan, but it was just as horrific. The water is becoming dark, and fog is surrounding the surface of it. Even a dark cloud forms in the sky, directly over whatever that thing is. "I knew I shouldn't have looked back," I say out loud.

I immediately stop running because I already know it's pointless. I turn one last time to see Karolyn disappear into the home near the outhouse. I take one deep breath to prepare myself for a fight before I turn around. "Here goes nothing," I utter as I rotate a hundred and eighty degrees to my right. To my surprise, this dark evil thing is standing motionless on the water's surface looking in my direction exactly the same as I'm looking at it. As a matter of fact, it kind of reminds me of............, "...Me," I say perplexingly! I squint to look closer, and it does the same. I move my right leg; it moves its left leg at the same time. I move my left; it moves its right. "This isn't right, and it doesn't feel right. Is this some type of evil mirror reflection of me," I ask? Suddenly, the truth slaps me right in the face. "I understand those flashes now, and the reason why I was transported to Rebecca's time. I was preordained to witness the evil powers that the skulls contain," I say with confidence.

When the Oracle recited that dream to me, he was actually providing me with the knowledge, of what the skulls were capable of; assisting a woman in the birth of an evil seed. In some cases, twin brothers would be born; one good and one evil. This is why I received those flashes of Cane killing his twin brother Abel, and Esau doing the same. Unfortunately, I couldn't stop Cane from killing Abel, but I did provide a means for Rebecca to prevent that future for her sons. "Is this what I've done for Karolyn also? Did I just stop her from touching the skull altogether? I believe so," I exclaim. In reality it's absolutely what I've done. When I first saw Karolyn, it seemed like an accident. However, it was really fate. I was meant to see something suspicious in her hand without knowing what it was at the time.

In the meantime, Satan on the other hand positioned the skull so that Karolyn would pick it up. However, by me traveling back in time, gaining this knowledge, and returning here; I prevented her from picking up that skull completely. This would eventually stop her from having an evil child, or twins in the future with one ultimately killing the other. As a matter of fact, it may stop her from having a child, period. "Hold up! Something just doesn't make sense to me. Why did Satan put it there and who keeps telling me to wake up," I ask frustratingly as that same voice speaks again?

"Close your eyes," the voice says. I finally respond to it while looking at that creature standing on the water. "No. Not yet. I'm not ready to," I end as I turn back around steady focusing on that thing. I expect it to do the same, but it doesn't. At this point, I'm lost because it was just mocking my every move, but now it isn't. Immediately, I turn my head, "Whatever," and start running towards the home Karolyn entered, hoping to move forward this time. I'm actually not running from that creature; I'm only trying to locate Karolyn to discover more facts about this whole situation. I believe that if Satan targeted her, then he must know something very important.

As I pick up the pace, the scenery finally moves past me. "Good. I guess all I had to do was listen to that little voice in my head and turn around, huh," I proclaim. Eventually, I start to approach the outhouse that she past earlier on my right side as I exit the woods. I begin to slow down without stopping to investigate it with my eyes, and then I continue until I reach the home ahead of me. As I round the corner on my left, I come to the front of the home, and there's a window that I can look through before reaching the porch. As I advance to look into the window, an adult man storms out of the door stumbling down the steps intoxicated, "I knew...knew I shouldn't have came back he...here woman," he stumbles on the ground slowly getting back up, "Youuu...aine nuthin," he pauses as he looks in my direction. I get nervous because I know what it looks like I'm doing right now; spying. But to my knowledge, he can't see me.

Just in case, I start to put my hands up and say, "Sir, I know...," but he cuts me off by continuing his rant. "And now you cheating on me... whh...wit that chap," he points in my direction. I turn around to see whose coming, and what I see is startling, "Nothing......Naaa. It's not possible. He can't...," I pause as an adult woman storms out of the house. She looks around and yells back at him, "Who Junnie, who? Ain't nobody out here but you and yo liqa botta. You always drinking, and you always talking 'bout leaving. Gone...Gone 'head. Leave," she points towards the end of the dirt road. He looks at me again, but his eyes tell me that he's accepting the fact that he's drunk and that I'm not really there. Then he stumbles off saying, "I will leave...an...an I won't com...come back no mo' 'till damarra...yyyy....you gone 'pologize to me," he pauses, and then starts slurring under his breath as he continues to wobble down the dirt road, "...Don't no woman......talk to no man lite dat." The lady walks back in the house and slams the wood door saying, "Don't make no sense. Always coming 'round starting some mess.

Won't try to get right," her voice fades out as she continues to argue. I look through the window to find Karolyn, but she's not around. All I see is two girls and one boy. They're young, but not too young; maybe between nine and fourteen. One of the girls looks older than the other two, until another walks around the corner. She actually looks to be between seventeen and nineteen. A bag swings over her shoulder as she turns to one of the girls and says, "I can't take this no mo. He always comin' round here screamin' and hollin; drunk. If Ma' asks where I'm at, tell her I'll be back. Annetta, you betta watch Karol and Stuie while I'm out. And Jeremiah, you look after your brother too. Don't let him get in no trouble when I'm gone; 'cause when I get back, it's gonna be you and his behind. You hear me?"

I look around trying to determine which one is Karol. At this moment I can't distinguish between them, but I can tell that the one giving orders is the same voice that I heard telling Karolyn not to go to the creek. This time it's just more mature. This means that one of these girls is Karolyn; unless she's in another room. That's when the girl that looks fourteen asks, "What about Jenny. Where she at?" The oldest one replies, "What I tell you 'bout asking questions, Annetta? Don't worry 'bout hu'; she sleep. She too young to get in yo' way, but nobody betta wake hu up neither," she ends as she walks out the door. She doesn't notice me at all as she trails down the dirt road whispering to herself, "I'mma miss ya'll, but I gotta get outta here."

I'm stunned because Karolyn was maybe six years old five minutes ago. And by what I just witnessed, "She has to be the girl that looks nine," I say softly. So far I've come to this conclusion because Annetta is the one that looks fourteen; Jeremiah is obviously the only boy standing there; Stuie is the other boy probably off playing somewhere; Jenny seems to be the youngest one of the bunch, and she's in the room asleep. That leaves only one person left, "Karol. That's her," I say enthusiastically as I hit the window on impulse. I'm so happy to see her again even though it's only been moments in my eyes, but years in hers. At the time I don't realize that Karolyn hears the thump on the glass. She doesn't necessarily walk towards it right at this moment, but I have caught her attention. She tilts her head, squints her eyes, and takes her first step towards the window at a normal pace.

I soon realize that she heard the knock on the window when she takes this step, but I also notice something strange happen as soon as her right foot touches the floorboard; time begins to move forward at a fast rate skipping days, or maybe even months ahead in this one step. Everyone's moving in and out of the house at a fast rate, but they are slowly aging according to the time change. However, Karolyn's forward momentum stays normal as she takes her next step. She only about four more steps away from the window when I start to think, “If time keeps skipping so far ahead with each one of her steps, I wonder how much older she will look when she reaches the glass.”

I duck down with my back to the wood so that she won’t be frightened if she sees me, but at the same time I want her to see me for whatever reasons. “How can I accomplish this if I already know that she’ll run from me like she did before,” I ask myself as she reaches the window. I can tell if she stopped moving because the leaves on the trees have fallen and completely flourished again, and the birds are flying at a normal speed. At this point in time, I can’t see exactly what she’s doing but I hear her say, “Hello. Is anybody there? Alright Stew-gee, stop playing games. It ain’t funny no mo’,” she ends. A short silence falls over the air while I continue to stoop down. I want to stand up, but I know that if I do, we will be face to face at the window and she will really be terrified. “O.k., I’ll slide up nice and slow until I can see her shadow. Then I’ll watch it until it looks like its moving away,” I think. Just as I’m about to inch upwards, time begins to speed forward again as if she’s walking like before. Then all of a sudden, the door opens, and out comes Karolyn saying, “Stew-gee, I’mma hurt you if you out here playing.”

I quickly get up as soon as I hear the door open because I know it’s her. I grab a stick from the ground on the way up, which oddly looks like the same stick from when I recorded the devil’s arrival, and I place it on the outside wind sill. Immediately I run around the corner as she takes her first step out of the door. Once she gets down the steps and walks towards the window, time slows to normal again. I begin saying to myself, “I hope that stick fulfills her curiosity on where the noise came from.”

I slowly peek around the corner to confirm that notion, but what I see is absolutely amazing. Karolyn has grown from a possible nine year old, to what now looks like a fourteen or fifteen year old. "Wow. That is simply amazing," I say to myself. At the same time, the ground rumbles very softly, but I pay no immediate attention to it. I keep my eyes on Karolyn as she looks around before actually walking towards the window. With each step that she takes, the ground rumbles and echoes accordingly, but harder with each step like a large monster coming towards us. The tremors become so vigorous that I turn to scan the area to look for signs of orientation. However, before I turn, I realize by analyzing Karolyn's body language that she remains clueless about these vibrations. She picks up the stick as I turn to look towards the wooded area where I exited from. I feel a strong gust of wind as trees within the woods begin to tumble over as if something is pushing them down while moving closer.

"Huh," Karolyn gasps. As soon as she respires, I see the monster exit the woods knocking down the last tree in its path. I say very softly under my breath, "It's that same creature that I left standing in the middle of the creek. Is it following me," I end? It stands at the edge of the last uprooted tree that it knocked over and begins to forcefully shake its body from only the waist up very quickly and disturbingly. As I continue to look at what seems to be involuntary body shudders from this thing, I failed to realize nature's volume dwindle to a dead silence.

Then out of nowhere comes an earsplitting plate scraping noise originating from that thing's location. "Aaahhhh," I utter out of absolute misery as I cover my ears while quickly bending over and closing my eyes from the excruciating pain. While stooped over, I turn my back towards the monster with my eyes still closed trying to cancel out as much of the noise as possible. However, this tactic isn't working. At this point, I've completely taken my mind off of Karolyn and can only think about moving as far away from this noise as possible, until...

...until I open my eyes towards the ground, still leaning over, realizing what I'm now looking at. "Feet...Karolyn...no," I gasp.

What I didn't realize is that Karolyn could hear the trees tumbling over even though she couldn't feel the vibrations of the monster's steps. To her, it was like a strong wind possibly rushed by and knocked over an old tree or two, and sequentially caused a domino effect with a few more. Her curiosity got the best of her again, and led her to walk around the corner of the house to investigate the commotion. As I scale up from her feet to her head, I notice that her face is pale and her eyes are focused straight ahead. She hasn't noticed me at all; at least from what I can tell. As the screeching noise silences, I remove my hands from my ears and slowly stand upright to face her. "Karolyn, I'm not here to...," I end my sentence quickly because I realize that she has no clue of my existence this time around. However, "What has she seen that's so frightening," I say to myself as I pause for a very short moment of silence. In this moment I trace her eyes in the direction in which they're staring and, "No...it can't be," I speak under my breath as my eyes again land upon that monster. "It can't be possible for her to see that thing."

The monster, still vibrating from waist up, suddenly disappears as time slows down dramatically for me. For Karolyn, it's still at normal speed. From my point of view, I see the monster relocate about six feet to the right of its previous location in a kneeling position. Its arms are spread out in front its right knee, hands touching the ground, and head down while the upper body remains shaking fiercely. This transfer occurred very quickly for my normal space time visual, but from Karolyn's standpoint it happened at lightning speed. The monster's head then forcefully yanks itself upward, without moving any of its other body parts, and stares in our direction for a short second. It then warps six feet to the left of that position with its waist up folded backwards, like someone had snapped its spine, while the half below remains vertical.

This is one the most disturbing things that I've seen thus far. On top of that, every time it warps it leaves behind a small crater of destruction in its previous location; along with a strong tremor of energy and a short terrifying screeching sound burst as it arrives to its new spot. When it teleports for the third time, I realize that it's advancing to our current location. "I have to protect Karolyn. But how," I utter as I begin to turn around catching a peripheral view of the creature in another strange position during my rotation? Simultaneously, time begins to return to normal speed.

"Close your eyes and wake up before it's too late," the voice says again. Upon facing Karolyn, I see her eyes closing and I hear that voice gradually transform into hers saying, "Wake up before it's too late. It's only a dream. Wake up," she keeps repeating. "Was she saying this to me the whole time, or is this a sign from God," I silently ask myself? As she opens her eyes hoping to be awake, my spirit begins to glow once more. I can tell that I'm now visible to her, because she quickly glances unbelievably back and forth in my eyes and the direction of that evil creature. She then gasps and yells out as her eyes become watery, "It's not a dream." The quakes and screeching sound waves become more frequent, meaning the monster is closing its distance between us while the next group of events happens at nearly the same time. First, as Karolyn's left hand rises to point in the direction of evil and her right hand collides with her face to cover her mouth, my spirit's energy begins to rapidly pulse and increase with each recurrence. At the same time, she quickly inhales deeply and releases a muffled scream that manages to escape her palm with a vengeance. As the last bit of sound exits her mouth and time slows to a snail's pace once more, she begins to lose consciousness from anxiety overload and wobbles from side to side.

By this time, I'm already reaching out to grab hold of her in hopes that I can become solid enough to actually touch and protect her. The ground is quaking so violently at this point that I'm thrown off balance as if I was being intentional pushed away from grabbing Karolyn. Fortunately, she's falling towards me instead of away, and I regain my ground at the appropriate time to attempt to catch her. Everything is happening in slow motion for me and the monster, but again for her it's normal. Amazingly, I'm able to grab her while my spirit pulses even stronger. While I'm holding Karolyn, I rotate only my head to see how close the monster has advanced during this short time which, by the way, would be slowing down for her as well if she was conscious enough to notice it. I turn to finally see this thing launch itself one last time from eight feet away to standing two feet directly behind me. Karolyn eyes are fully closed which signals to me that she has completely passed out at this point. The monster arches back and spreads out both of its arms to attack us as I begin to close my eyes to the rhythm of time quickly speeding back up while I praying. Just before my eyes close entirely, the last things I see are a pair of hands one centimeter away from my eyelashes and the mouth of this thing horrifically opened wide about to release another one of it's screeching sound bursts. However, the last things I feel are the ground collapsing beneath my feet from the crater the monster forms with its destructive arrival, and a pulse being released from my spirit that feels as though it's carrying the force of a supernova explosion.

As I begin to fall forward from the loss of balance, Karolyn remains unconscious in my arms while she, on the other hand, is falling backwards. The last thing I hear is the scream of a monster being deteriorated by the power of my energy surge as I begin to pray for Karolyn. But, "Something isn't right. We're still falling," I think to myself as I force my eyes closed even harder than they already are.

At this point, I start to pray to myself for Karolyn more intensely. However, we keep falling as though there's no ground to touch at all as her shirt continues to tap at my arm from the gushing breeze of us now reaching a free fall status. “Is it possible that this thing was smart enough to create an abyss beneath us as a last resort in case it didn’t succeed at destroying us with its bare hands,” I think while continuing to contemplate with my eyes closed? Eventually I open my eyes to face this nonstop fall head on and protect Karolyn from what I can see. But what I see is nothing but...

Chapter 7: Obscurity: Eliminate the Darkness and Follow the Path...of Glory to...

I can't even see Karolyn in front of me even though I can still feel her in my arms. If I didn't know any better, I would believe my eyes were still closed. Suddenly, the wind becomes more powerful, and is now pushing downwards on my back equally the same as upwards on Karolyn's back. The force is so strong that it appears to be merging us together as one spirit. I literally feel like I'm absorbing her essence, and so I begin to panic because destroying her is the last thing I want to do. "Karolyn, wake up. You have to wake up right now," I yell unsuccessfully as the feeling of her body completely dissolves into my spirit.

"Please, Karoly...Uugh," I express from the sudden impact of what feels like water. My sight returns at the exact point of impact with this large body of, "Red water," I manage to gurgle underwater as I get a glance of red bubbles entering my vision. I have no clue of where Karolyn is, and being able to see only one foot in front of me in a three hundred and sixty degree radius isn't helping either. I flap my arms to help me float to the surface expecting to see more clearly as I rise to the top; however, reaching the top isn't as close as I originally thought it was. Everything remains consistently dark outside of my one foot range as I continue to flail my arms up and down. For some strange reason I feel as though I'm being drained of energy, at the same time able to breathe just enough to help me survive below the surface for little while. Though it feels like I will run out of breath with each second that passes. It's almost like this red water is trying to kill me. As I continue upwards, something nudges my left leg. "Huh," I utter as I look down trying to see past my chest. Just as quickly something nudges my right foot, and then my left again. I flail even harder at the same time wondering, "Why is it taking so long to reach the top," and, "If I can feel something scrubbing past my feet, then it has to feel me too," I end.

I try my hardest to get to the top before something that I can't see starts to attack me. But then I quickly came to my senses, "This is another one of Satan's tricks," I again gurgle my words underwater as I remembered something that Alpha said to me previously. "Do not be afraid even of evil, because only then can he harm you. Otherwise, he can only try to influence his surroundings," Alpha's voice echoes within my spirit. I feel reassured and say to myself, "I know what I must do. I have to...

I begin to pray to myself the same words that helped you banish Satan from your body earlier, "You must find a way to weaken the spirit by damaging the body hoping to confuse the Will. Then you destroy the spirit to control the mind and body," I pause look upwards and continue, "You have no power here, Satan. I have figured out your deceitful game. You tried to make me think that Karolyn is gone, but she was never here in the first place. I saved her and she is where she supposed to be right now." As I continue to look up, my area of sight gradually expands beyond ten feet, then twenty, and so on and so forth. My vision apparently corresponds to my faith in God. But Satan doesn't stop here. The area below my feet begins to bubble as if it was boiling. As I look down, I see the same monster that I thought had been destroyed before I fell here, swimming in circles around my feet. What becomes even stranger is that it divides into two identical fiends. Then those two multiply twice until this process creates what appears to be hundreds of these creatures grabbing at me feet to pull down. At first glance I was startled, but then I continue as the water bubbles more violently, "But I have a strong Will, and you have no home here," I end as I begin to ascend to the surface at an alarming rate like I had been shot out something very powerful.

Of course those creatures are narrowly on my trail without me having to look down to observe it. As my vision continues to now stretch outwards for miles, I begin to see a very vague depiction of the surface. I have my full attention on reaching the top with no thoughts of ever looking down again, until I hear a deep and angry voice come from below, "You insect.

I have defied the so called almighty's will. No one has a stronger will than me," Satan proclaims. This of course causes me to look down out of curiosity. At first I still see the multitude of demons hounding me, but that suddenly changes. I witness one fiend get yanked out of the way very ferociously by a force that I can't see at this moment. Then another, until eventually I see the face of Karolyn clawing her way above them all. As I gain distance between myself and those creatures, Karolyn reaches up towards me while I hear her voice in my head helplessly say, "Help me. Don't leave me hear." By this time, all the tricks that Satan could possibly play, this one was the most absurd.

I say out loud in response to his game, "You have no place here," I end as I look back towards the surface. Karolyn's image quickly converts into his as he becomes more frustrated. I'm too far away for him to attempt to catch up, and I'm to close to the surface to even care anymore; until, "Uuuuuuaaahhh," Satan grunts as he blasts upwards at an underwater supersonic speed instantly disintegrating most of the demons surrounding him. "Do you really think you can escape me," he screams as he begins to twirl at a startling rate. "If you won't come to me, then I'll bring you to me," he declares.

The force from him twirling upwards at that speed forms a massive whirlpool in little or no time at all. However, I keep myself focused even when the current reaches my location and slowly attempts to pull me under. "You must find a way to weaken the spirit. You must find a way to weaken the spirit," I keep repeating to stay focused. I'm now two feet below the surface and can see a beautiful blue light above so close to me that I can almost touch it. However, at this point the strength of the good in me and his evil powers begins to clash to a point where my ascension becomes a stalemate. The full current from the whirlpool hasn't completely reached me, but it's strong enough to hold me at a standstill.

However, I maintain confidence as I look down one last time to see Satan accelerating upwards through the middle of the whirlpool reaching out with his left hand to grab me. He's still a good ways away increasing in size as he nears, but the whirlpool is very close. If the current continues to gain strength and he continues to close proximity, then he will reach me before I get to the surface. As the bulk of the whirlpool nears me and he grunts for the final time, I say out loud, "You have no place here, Satan. My body is my father's house and law. Alpha's Will be done," I end as I close my eyes in faith. While the current becomes almost unbearable, I hear Alpha's voice say, "You have reached the end of the beginning willingly. Since have chosen your path by eliminating the darkness to reach the surface, you are now beginning the end. Reach up, pull yourself out of these dangerous waters,..."

As I reach up to pull myself out of the water, Satan continues to advance through the whirlpool's center at his full potential in hopes to grab me and pull me down before I exit. I can hear his voice echo very loud and deeply, "This is only the beginning, Seer. There's no way to ever escape me," he laughs as I finally pull the upper half of my body out of this deadly red water. As usual, to my surprise, half of my body is located above a spotless clear but white floor that seems to expand indefinitely. However, the other half below this strange floor remains under water. I can still sense the strong current from the whirlpool below and Satan's presence getting closer.

I completely pull myself out of the floor and water at the same time, and I'm instantly standing in front of a white ladder that seems to reach to the heavens from what I can see. However, there are so many people on it that the ladder itself is barely visible, and they all seem to be either afraid to climb all the way up or purposely blocking someone else's path to the top. If I wasn't such an analytical type of person, my first deduction would've been a human ladder that reaches Himil. Anyhow, they all seem to be talking about something to each other or to themselves at the same time, which winds up being loud mumbling from the mix of all the voices.

As I take one step forward, the ground rumbles dramatically and suddenly, "Aaarrghh," Satan's voice breaches the floor followed by his right hand forcefully extending through it directly behind me. I immediately turn around to witness small pieces of rubble being expelled outwards in all direction. The quake from his forceful entry shakes the ladder tremendously causing two people to fall from an unseen portion of it. Their screams warn me to look up, and my instincts force me to jump to the right to escape their deadly impacts from that distance. They crash land straight through the floor and into the water beneath me. I watch them trying to swim back to the surface as the floor quickly fuses back together. They almost make it to top, but are unfortunately converted into the same demons that seemed to be circling me as I swam up. Simultaneously, Satan's left hand bursts through the floor directly beneath me and manages to grab my right ankle. Unfortunately for him, his presence is not allowed in this null zone which is something I don't know at this time.

"You'll never be safe," Satan's voice rumbles as both of his arms begin to fade away while his left hand still holds my ankle. Again, the opening in the broken floor begins to repair itself with loose fragments almost as quickly as his arms entered. He finally vanishes as I turn back towards the ladder saying, "Wow. What persistence." At this point, I'm more curious about where I am than climbing up this human swamped ladder. "This must be a place that Satan is not allowed to journey within based on my synopsis of what just happened. But where or what is it," I say as I do a quick scan of the area behind the ladder again just to make sure of what I saw earlier. "Yep! Nothing but floor," I say softly as I shake my head from side to side. As the incoherent and noisy chattering from everyone continues, I look up wondering, "How am I supposed to get through all of these people," I think to myself for split second. "You know, maybe I don't have to climb up. Maybe I can keep walking until I reach something else," I ponder as I walk around the ladder to bypass it all. Surprised yet again, the ladder moves along with my every step. I begin to sprint and turn in all directions to try to lose it, but it remains at the right of me. "You got to be kidding me. There's no way around it. I guess I have to climb up if I want to get out of here, huh," questioning myself in a sort of frustrating manner?

As I look up to give a quick eye measurement of how far I have to climb, I witness six more people fall from high above and straight through the floor. They too are transformed into demon-like creatures. To no avail, Satan tries to quickly breach the holes that were created by them before they close. I shake my head and say, "O.k. falling isn't an option. This means I definitely have to reach to top. No questions asked," I end as I begin my climb. I can't grab any portion of the ladder, so I do the next best thing; I use the people as stepping tools. At the same time, I'm also making sure that I keep a tight grip on my way up. I would hate to end up like the others.

Trying to conserve energy by keeping a normal pace, I overhear a random voice from someone above yell out, "There's no end. There's no top." At this moment, two other people fall from high above. As they near my vicinity, they both try to grab someone else on the ladder to keep from plummeting to the bottom. With these actions, they end up taking five more victims with them. Each one of them tried to grab someone to fall with them, or at least to stop their descent. One person actually manages to snag someone else and sequentially stops his fall. The other six continue through the floor. This scenario continues as hours and hours seem to pass by. I try not to look up or down because this may decrease my expectations of reaching the top.

Although, I came close to falling at least seven times as a result of someone else's errors. As more time passes by, I finally decide to look up to calculate the remaining distance. Once again I'm disappointed. This forces me to look down to measure how far I've traveled. What I see at this point causes me to involuntarily scream from frustration, "You've got to be kidding me. I've been traveling this far, and I'm still in the same place. It's not possible. There's just no way..," I continue to rant uncontrollably. By this time, my body is exhausted from climbing. At any moment I feel as though I will lose my grip. "I have to rest a while," I say to myself as I hold on to the nearest person as tight as possible. I would love to take a nap, "No, that wouldn't be a good idea," I think as my eyes begin to close on their own.

Silence begins to cloak time and space, and I feel like I'm becoming trapped in a dream. Somehow, my own voice echoes in my head, "Faith...faith is the key." I immediately open my eyes at the exact moment I lose my grip. I begin to fall at a rapid pace, and should hit the ground at any moment. However, instead of panicking, screaming, and trying to take the others with me; I fearlessly spread my arms out as I continue to fall backwards towards the ground while thinking, "I will not take anyone else with me. This is my failed journey," I end at the same time I hit the ground. The impact knocks me unconscious for at least a minute or so, but in this minute I'm taught a very valuable lesson by Alpha. "The same way you fall down, you fall up. Despair topples the mightiest of all the mighty, but only through faith shall you ascend," Alpha ends as I begin to regain consciousness.

When I fully awaken, I'm looking straight up to the sky with blurry vision. However, I see no ladder or people in my immediate line of sight. On the other hand, I feel my arms dangling over the edge of whatever I'm on. I take a deep breath expecting to fight Satan any moment now, but as I continue to regain focus, I notice that I'm not in the water. I begin to lean up, but I quickly lay back down to avoid a collision with someone jumping over me from my feet to my head. I haven't had a chance to see what I'm laying on, but as the person lands, it slightly sways from side to side.

"What in the world," I say under my breath. As I cautiously bring myself to a sitting position this time around, I realize that I'm sitting on top of a long wooden lath of some sort. This board is only about the width of my body, but seems to be very long and unstable. I can see that at the end of where I'm looking, at this moment, is the same ladder that I tried to climb. "But how did I...," I quickly cut myself off. From Alpha's words echoing in my head, I instantly knew what had occurred. The only way to reach the top of the ladder is on pure faith. There's no way to reach it by climbing up on your own strength because you will eventually bring someone down in the process. Only by allowing God's Will to carry you to the top, is it become possible.

"That explains why so many people were just barely holding on and then tried to take somebody with them when they fell. They were trying to do whatever it took to get to the top, or to stay where they were," I utter. With this analysis, I begin to understand exactly what this place is. "So this place is a null void. A neutral zone. A place where we make a choice without any interference from God or Satan," I end. I was exactly right. That's the sole reason why Satan's presence was rejected when I reached the surface, and why I didn't hear God's voice until I made the right choice. And for the one's who made the wrong choice, that's why they were converted into demons and not allowed back into this zone. “I actually get it. If you can fall down, why can’t you fall up? But where do I go from here,” I ask myself.

I stand completely up and scan the immediate area in front of me one last time before I turn around. I do this to make sure that I don’t miss any clues that may possibly help me. I actually see people inches from the top of the ladder, but I can tell that they don’t realize where they are because of how they’re holding on. I carefully take a few steps on this wobbly board towards them in hopes to help a couple of them to the top, but with each step the distance becomes further by triple the amount. “I take that as a no,” I say out loud. With great balance and focus, I gently turn around one hundred and eighty degrees. What I see at this point is astonishing. A few feet in front of me is an enormous red brick wall that reaches infinity both height and width. The height begins at the edge of the platform. As I trace it with my eyes, I notice a strange figure with its arms folded seemingly trapped inside of the bricks. If it hadn’t moved its eyes, I would’ve missed it completely. “This is too extraordinary. Either that is an enormous being camouflaged to match the wall, or it’s actually merged with the wall,” I think to myself. “My God. That’s an angel. A huuuge angel! I can see the wings. At least as far as the wall stretches,” I proclaim. This angel had to be nearly twenty to thirty feet tall with a wing span of forever. I immediately turn my attention to the person standing at the edge of the wall. “That’s the same person that jumped over me when I leaned up the first time. Why is he just standing there like a zombie? Is he afraid,” I ask myself?

I continue to watch as this person begins to walk into the wall as if doesn’t exist. His entrance resembled a person walking into a wall of water. I waste no time in refocusing my attention back at the angel in the wall. It remains motionless by only watching with its eyes. “This must be what I have to do,” I mumble. Confident in this decision, I slowly but surely inch my way to the edge of the wall trying to maintain my balance on this thin plank. "Don't look down, don't look down," I continuously chant to myself while I continue. It's very challenging, but I manage to make it to the edge of the wall. I look up at the angel hoping that it will provide some sort of guidance on what to do. However, it doesn't say a single word. "Excuse me. Hey. Heeeeyyyy," I continue until the angel unfolds its arms and bends over to acknowledge my provocations. It still doesn't say a word; however, it stares me directly in the eyes as I ask, "May I walk through your wall." The angel stands back up while saying in a tremendous voice that rumbles everything, "If it's your time."

"What? If it's my time? What does that mean," I ask confusingly? Unfortunately, the angel does not respond anymore. "I guess I'll have to find out the hard way," I say softly as I rub my eyes and face with my right hand. Trying to build my confidence up, I stare at the wall for a short period before I decide to move. "Here goes nothing," I say as I quickly walk towards the wall and unexpectedly ram it. The wall even appears to forcefully push me the opposite way causing me to become unstable on the plank. To make the situation worse, someone else takes the leap of faith and violently lands on the plank. This person obviously figured out how to get to the top of the ladder as well; however, with extremely bad timing. This landing jolted the board at the same time that I stumble backwards causing me to become very unbalanced.

At this point, I'm weaving back and with my arms flailing back and forth like a bird flapping its wings. To top it off, three more people take the leap of faith and land at nearly the same time. This complicated situations to the extreme by tilting the board, bouncing the first person in the air and over the edge, and forcing me and everyone else over the edge as well. Everyone in this situation had quick enough reflexes to grab the edge of the board instinctively on different sides of the plank. Three people are on one side and three are on the other. It actually balances out. On the other hand, the circumstances become very hectic due to the fact that we all have loose grips with only one hand holding on. I hastily reach up to grab the edge with my right hand while I observe the others do the same. We all attempt to pull ourselves up at nearly the same time. I am the first to make it to the top, and I immediately begin to position my body to help stabilizes the board for the others. Two more peoplemanage to pull themselves up soon after, but cause another shift in balance because of their positions. This forces the other three to lose their grips and plummet to the bottom.

"Noooo. But they made it," I scream out as they fall. The only thing left to do at this moment is find a way through this wall as soon as possible before anyone else falls and throws us off balance again. I carefully turn around to face the wall for the second time as I take a deep breath and close my eyes. "If I made it this far with faith, then I'll continue with faith," I say out loud as I release all nervousness and fear of falling. In this moment of concentration, I meditate on how many times I've forgot to grasp my faith because of loss of focus on this strange journey. Then I think about the possibilities of why. "Maybe because I'm prone to make mistakes? I don't know, but it's faith from here on out," I end with a reconfirmed confidence.

With my eyes remaining closed, I completely blank out any thoughts of failure at this point and take an enormous step with my right leg towards the wall on strictly faith. Another person hits the lath before my foot touches it, and forces it to rock back and forth while becoming lopsided. However, I continue forward unfazed by the impact, almost as if I'm walking on air. As I continue forward, I feel my body begin to merge with the wall. It actually feels like I'm walking through thick pressurized water. The same brick angel appears behind my eyelids smiling from ear to ear and says while kneeling over, "It's your time." On the flipside, the angel remains motionless and only moves its eyes.

I keep my eyes closed as it grabs my hand and walks me through to the other side. The image of the angel disappears as soon as I come to a complete stop. When I finally open my eyes, I expect to begin in heaven or at least somewhere with a lot of angels. Instead, I find myself in a gymnasium that goes on for miles and miles. The floor is painted and tiled with the same color and material as an orange basketball. On the left side of me are small and very old condemned looking churches that continue to multiply until unseen, and on the right side is nothing. "Wow! Now that's completely unexpected," I say with a smile on my face very close to laughing.

As I look around while walking forward I say to myself, "I guess I have to pick a church. But which one do I choose," I ask? "My faith will show me the right path," I continue forward with haste waiting to receive a sign for the correct church to enter. I'm determined not to stop walking until I get a gut feeling of some sort. Days seem to pass by, but I know that time differs in these zones which means it may only be seconds. As I continue moving, I pass hundreds of churches, but not one signal to stop at any one of them. I even pick up the pace a little. However, I'm not anxious to receive a message or enter one of these churches. I'm just enjoying myself because I made it past all of these trials and obstacles that the devil placed in my path. With this thought passing through my mind, I even started skipping and whistling on my way. "I know God will lead me down the right path," I say out loud with pride.

No sooner than I finished this sentence, I witness a different scenery appear on the horizon. I can't make out exactly what it is at this point, but it did give me a gut feeling. "That must be where I have to stop," I say as I begin to sprint towards my destination. As I get closer to my objective, one image becomes hundreds. Then those hundreds become thousands until I realize what I'm looking at. These images finally appear as people standing in a long line one after the other for whatever reasons. Right now, I can't see what they're standing in line for, but it must be seriously important. "Not important enough for me to stand in line waiting though," I exclaim. I deduce that it can't be one of these churches to my left, because there's no line for them. "Well, it could be the gates of Himil at the end of the line. But my faith is telling me that it's just something else," I end without any negative or bad thoughts. Although I do recognize something as I come up behind the last person in line. "That's the same man that jumped over me and walked through the wall before I did," I utter with curiosity. I slow my sprint to a walking pace as I pass him, but what I notice isn't what I expect. As I near his left shoulder, I can't help but note the look in his eyes. "Is he in a trance, or what," I silently ask myself?

He doesn't seem to notice me at all, so I stop in between him and the person ahead of him to wave my right hand in front of his face. Either he doesn't notice me at all, or maybe he has no intentions to acknowledge my gesture. "Well whatever it is...this isn't the line I need to stop in. But I still feel like I have a reason for being here," I end while I continue forward. As I pick up the pace again, I notice that everyone has the same expressions on their faces. Once more, days seem to pass by before I even slightly begin to see the front of the line. This is when I realize that these people are trying to enter one of these churches because I actually see the line curve into one. "Well, I guess I was wrong. Maybe I should be here too," I say out loud and continue forward almost a meter from the entrance. I take a quick look back and say, "Wow! That's a lot of people, and a long line to wait in though. Must be a good church! It sure is a lot bigger and flashier than the rest, and it looks new. But am I sure that I need to be here...," I turn back around and continue, "What does my faith say," I ask as I close my eyes to meditate? I continue to walk forward very slowly with my eyes closed until I hear my own inner voice echo loudly, "Stop. Just look up, and you'll see your reason for being here...but not like them." I stop walking and open my eyes. I very slowly trace the church's foundation all the way to the top of the steeple.

"What am I looking f...," I quickly cut myself off and continue with, "...oh...my...God! But how," I ask with much confusion? I see an uncountable number of demons flying around the battlement of the church with a few mounted on it. Many of them are looking down at everyone trying to enter the church. As I continue to investigate the demon filled sky above, I notice one of them look down at me. I even hear his demonic voice from high up say in a language that I don't understand, "He doesn't belong here," he ends while pointing down towards me to warn the other demons. However, none of them try to pursue me at this point. I formulate a really good explanation why too.

I begin calculating those reasons to myself as I start to walk towards the ushers at the double door entrance, "They can't touch down in their demonic states, because if these people see them like this, then they will flee from fear. However, they can maintain full control over these people as long as they don't show their true image or cause any unnecessary ruckus that would be disrespectful to how a church is perceived to be," I pause and then continue as I figure out something else, "That's why I couldn't break that guy's trance. He was already caught up and chose to disconnect his mind from any outside protests or interruptions...huh...Satan attacked his spirit and is now controlling his mind like the rest of these people," I pause my thinking for a split second as I get about fifteen feet from the entrance.

"But I thought that if you walked through the wall, you were good to go," I end as I finally come to a conclusion that Satan will not stop until you reach Himil itself. He did say that earlier on, so I can only speculate that he was really serious about it too. I step up to the two ushers at the entrance dressed in all white including their gloves. They actually look like normal people from what I can see at the moment. However, when the usher to my left presents a pamphlet, he says, "Welcome to BB, CC, JJ, and TZ HISS, Brother," he ends very enthusiastically. The one on the right immediately responds, "We hope you decide to stay with us. You're always welcomed here." Even though I don't know what those acronyms stand for, I still reject the pamphlet, lean forward in the middle of both ushers, touch their outside shoulders with each hand, and say, "If he won't stop, then neither will I," I end as they both look at me at the exact same time. Their faces quickly flash their true appearances with red eyes and then return to normal. No one in line seems to pay attention to me or them, so I casually remove my hands and walk inside.

The minute I step foot into the building, everyone sitting down turns around to acknowledge my entrance as one of their brothers. Each of their eyes flashes red except one familiar looking lady sitting in the front on the floor up against the wall. Obviously, it's too late for everyone else except her. "This is why I'm here; to bring her out before it's too late. The same way that Satan has penetrated this church to bring these people in, I'll infiltrate it to bring someone out," I think to myself as I begin to walk from the back to the front where she's located. I'm careful not to walk down the aisles because I don't want to draw too much attention to myself before I reach her. At this time everyone returns to their normal sitting positions to heed the word that's being spoken.

There's a Vicar at the pulpit with a man standing to her left. I assume this is her husband. I come to this determination because she's the one that's preaching while he's sitting down, and they have on similar white robes. There's also a full choir, instruments and all, directly behind them dressed in white and blue robes. There are also three men in a group to the right of the Vicar and three women in a group to the left of her husband. On the wall behind them reads the title of the church, "Baha'i, Buddhism,

Christianity, Confucianism, Judaism, Jainism, Taoism, Zoroastrianism, Hinduism, Islam, Shinto, and Sikhism. When I see this, I think to myself, "I figured out what BB, CC, JJ, and TZ HISS stands for. Boy he's brave. He's telling them what he's doing, and they still don't get it," I end my thoughts as I finally make it to the front. On the way up, I thought I saw two more people that I recognized sitting in the back. Anyhow, I sit down on the floor next to lady. She's sitting with her back against the wall and her arms hugging her knees, and we're both directly aligned about thirty feet horizontally to the left of the Vicar's location.

A huge black speaker is partially blocking my view of the pulpit, so I'm sure that this lady can't see it at all. "Welcome, Brother. My name is Shalamamababa, Nrronictoo, Shalamamababa," she continues as she begins to rock back and forth while raising her hands in the air. I have no clue what she's saying, but at the same time, I notice most of the church doing and saying the same things. Some people are even up jumping around. I look back towards the Vicar and notice that she and her husband, now standing, are both leaning past the view of the speaker and looking directly at me. I take it that they're trying to figure out whether or not I'm one of them. At this time, I hear my inner voice say, "You better not participate. You just watch. The next time you get up will be when you walk out of here." Immediately, without even looking at me, the lady grabs my knee with her left hand and says, "Help me." I ignore her for the moment because I'm more worried about why everyone on the pulpit has just now turned their eyes towards me. The Vicar continues to preach with her eyes planted on me saying, "Please turn in your books to the beginning, Chapter 11."

As I look around, I see everyone with books except this lady. The Vicar begins to read from the book without even looking at it. She and her husband are still looking at me as they both recite at the same time, "Now the whole earth had one language and the same words...," they continue as I notice that this lady is saying the same thing, with her head now in between her knees, without a book to read from. That's when I realized that they weren't looking at me; they were looking at her and trying to force a full crossover. The lady continues at the same time almost as if she was the puppet and the Vicar was the ventriloquist, "...they came upon a plain in the land of Shinar and settled. And they said to each other, 'Come, let us build ourselves a city, and a tower with its top in the heavens, and let us make a name for ourselves. If we don't, then we shall be scattered upon the face of the whole earth," she ends and starts shaking violently. She grabs my knee tighter and says again, "Help me."

The Vicar knows that it's possible to lose her, so she announces, "Everybody bow your heads. Let us pray," she ends as everyone in the church bows their head except the people on the pulpit. They continue to look in our direction. By this time, the lady has a face full of tears and bows her head to comply. With all of this happening at one time, I just realized a few more things to add to my collection from this journey. This particular church isn't right, and that means everything that they do in here isn't right, including bowing their heads. Instead of bowing my head, I look up and begin to silently pray, "God, I just now realized that all this time of bowing my head to pray, I've been disrespecting your power. Satan has always been represented as being below and you above. Why would I ever look down on you? This only means that I've been looking up to Satan this whole time. Please forgive me for unknowingly praying to the deceitful one. I guess he found a way to get to you even with the littlest things. From now on, I will be looking up to you...literally and physically when I pray. You are the almighty, and I will do it proudly," I end with my head still to the sky.

By this time, mostly everyone in the church is speaking in a language that I can't understand, including the Vicar and this lady.

It doesn't take them long to regain control of her because she removes her hand from my knee as a strange book begins to appear in front of her feet while she recites the passages on the Vicar's command, "The Lord came down to see the city and the tower, which mortals had built, and said, 'Look, they are one people, and they have all one language; and this is only the beginning of what they will do; nothing that they propose to do will now be impossible for them.'," the Vicar, along with her husband, quickly pauses and looks at me. The reason their attention is redirected towards me, is because I suddenly receive this huge rush of adrenaline from an unseen source that makes me shake shortly like a cold chill while my head remains to the sky. This wasn't a normal action in this church, and so they were now really focused on me, and their actions cause some of the members to look in my direction as well. The Almighty's voice enters my head and repeats the phrase, "I am not the God of confusion.

You have realized the difference between right and wrong. There's a thin line between many things. But there is no line between Me and Him. It's just good or bad; no in betweens. It takes a strong will to know and accept this. Then, and only then, are you able to speak on it," Alpha ends. I regain focus and finally notice that all eyes are on me. I quickly look down at the lady as I stand up to leave this unholy place. Once I completely stand to my feet, I kneel over to pick her up for a hasty exit. She's completely out of it at this point, but somehow finds the strength to fight the Vicar's control and say, "Help me." The book slowly fades away as the husband begins to cautiously walk in my direction while most of the people stand to their feet.

The Vicar continues reciting the script trying to hold on to this lady's Will, as she now becomes a puppet rejecting her master, "The Lord came down to see the city and the tower, which mortals had built. And the Lord said, 'Look, they are one people, and they have all one language; and this is only the beginning of what they will do; nothing that they propose to do will now be impossible for them..." the lady begins to stutter the words. She's slowly but surely breaking away as I continue to walk quickly with her in my arms towards the entrance.

The Vicar continues to try as her husband moves faster to catch up, "Come, let us go down, and confuse their language there, so that they will not understand one another's speech," she ends because the lady did not repeat this part of the passage. As we near the door, the Vicar becomes frustrated and yells, "Don't let them leave." Her husband is in an all-out sprint and has come within a ten foot range as he shouts, "Stop them." The members are all mumbling in disarray with some clearly contemplated an attack. I'm not at all worried because I know that we are too close to the door, and if my earlier judgment serves me right; no one will make a move now that I'm visible to the line outside. They will not want to deter the millions and millions of people for just two people trying to leave.

Then, suddenly, two voices speak at once, perfectly synchronized. One is unmistakably Alpha. The other is not. "You're doing great. Try one more time… I promise—" The voices merge, then separate. Only Alpha remains. "…Wajolebe." At the sound of my name, I inhale sharply. My body reacts before I can think. I begin to open my eyes slowly, fighting against the overwhelming brightness. And as I do, the two voices merge once more, completing the sentence: "…it will be…"

Without hesitation, I reach forward again, but before I can make contact, an overwhelming pressure crashes down onto my shoulders. The weight shifts. It is no longer just her. It feels as though something far heavier has taken hold, pressing me down from both sides. I cannot lift my arms. I cannot move. It feels like I am being crushed, yet there is no pain. "I can't push," I say aloud. "I can't even move." I am not afraid, but I am concerned. If I cannot move forward, how can I fulfill what I was meant to do? The light behind my eyes grows stronger, brighter than ever.

Instantly, the barrier releases my hand. The light intensifies as if the sun itself is rising behind my eyelids. I attempt to open my eyes, but something holds them closed. Then I remember: I have only heard my name once. So I wait. I lower my hand and adjust my stance, balancing the woman on my shoulder. Suddenly, a surge of energy moves through me, filled with excitement, urgency, and purpose. "I remember!" I shout. "But what must I do to pass through this trial?" The response is immediate. "Push. Just push."

Fragments of what I was told echo through me, not in sequence, but all at once. "Try imagining emptiness… no sound… no time… You simply are… and it simply is…" Then another remembrance follows: "Yes… this is what I am… but this is not easy for you to comprehend…" As the realization deepens, a thought forms within me. This is what I was shown in the beginning, so why does it feel like the end? Is it because Alpha is Omega, and Omega is Alpha? The moment that thought settles, something within me shifts. A new awareness is born. Then I hear it again: "Take note of what you witness. This will be the first of many times I allow you to see in this way. Now journey toward Eden and prepare to open your eyes forward. You will become the narrator. Speak as yourself. No one will silence your voice or your knowledge. Listen for your name. When you hear it again, restore your sight."

As I attempt to pull my hand back, it resists. It does not let go. It is as if my hand has been fused to it. Then something changes. Behind my closed eyes, I begin to see light, faint at first, then growing. With that light comes understanding. Not thoughts, but realizations. Everything I have been taught since the beginning begins to surface all at once. It feels as though I have been elevated, granted the ability to translate light into sound, sound into meaning, and meaning into awareness. Clarity replaces confusion. Peace replaces uncertainty. I understand now. This is it.

Just as quickly as the world turned white, it turns dark. Not dim, but completely void. It is so dark that I cannot see anything, not even the woman in my arms. I try to focus, straining my eyes and bringing her closer, but nothing appears. Only emptiness. At that point, I close my eyes. There is no point in keeping them open. The instant I do, I hear my name once. Clear. Close. I do not respond. Instead, I shift her weight onto my left shoulder, freeing my right hand. With my eyes still closed, I extend my arm forward and feel something: a surface, a barrier. I trace it, slowly turning in a full circle. It surrounds me completely. Protection.

As I approach the exit, two things happen. First, I notice something shifting outside. Some of the people are no longer under the devil's influence. Whether this has anything to do with me, I don't know. Some stand frozen, looking around in confusion. Others move cautiously, waving their hands in front of unfamiliar faces, testing reality. Small conversations begin to form, quiet at first, uncertain, but spreading. Whatever broke their trance is spreading quickly. A chain reaction has begun. Then the second thing happens. The moment my foot crosses the threshold, everything disappears. Everything except her. She remains unconscious in my arms. Now it is just the two of us walking through an endless void. There is no ground, yet I can feel myself walking. No sky, no horizon, only white stretching infinitely in all directions. No distinction between above and below. "Am I walking through purgatory?"

The woman begins to speak in frantic, incoherent bursts. "People have come… they've tried to make me leave this church. We won't be able to exit. You're no different…" Her voice trails off as she suddenly collapses. At that exact moment, the Vicar's husband grips my shoulder with his left hand, stopping me in my tracks. His voice lowers to a whisper. "You're lucky to have made it this far... but nobody leaves." He begins pulling me back. Before he can take another step, the Vicar shouts sharply, "Let them leave. We are awaiting service." There's intention behind her command. She understands that if he continues to restrain us, it may draw attention strong enough to break the trance of those waiting outside. And if one mind breaks free, others may follow. That is a risk she is unwilling to take. To counter the growing disturbance, she signals the choir and band. Instantly, music erupts loud and overwhelming, meant to drown out the murmurs rising among the congregation. The husband loosens his grip and forces a smile. "For the sake of the church...please come back and visit us again, brother. You're always welcome here." The ushers step aside. Together, they say in unison, "Come again."

As I approach the exit, two things happen. First, I notice something shifting outside. Some of the people are no longer under the devil's influence. Whether this has anything to do with me, I don't know. Some stand frozen, looking around in confusion. Others move cautiously, waving their hands in front of unfamiliar faces, testing reality. Small conversations begin to form quiet at first, uncertain but spreading. Whatever broke their trance is spreading quickly. A chain reaction has begun. Then the second thing happens. The moment my foot crosses the threshold, everything disappears. Everything...except her. She remains unconscious in my arms. Now it's just the two of us walking through an endless void. There is no ground, yet I can feel myself walking. No sky, no horizon only white, stretching infinitely in all directions. No distinction between above and below. "Am I walking through purgatory?"

Just as quickly as the world turned white...it turns dark. Not dim, but completely void. So dark that I cannot see anything, not even the woman in my arms. I try to focus, straining my eyes, bringing her closer but nothing appears. Only emptiness. At that point, I close my eyes. There's no point in keeping them open. The instant I do, I hear my name. Once. Clear. Close. I don't respond. Instead, I shift her weight onto my left shoulder, freeing my right hand. With my eyes still closed, I extend my arm forward and feel something. A surface. A barrier. I trace it, slowly turning in a full circle. It surrounds me completely. Protection.

As I attempt to pull my hand back, it resists. It doesn't let go. It's as if my hand has been fused to it. Then… something changes. Behind my closed eyes, I begin to see light. Faint at first then growing. With that light comes understanding. Not thoughts…but realizations. Everything I've been taught since the beginning begins to surface all at once. It feels as though I've been elevated granted the ability to translate light into sound, sound into meaning, and meaning into awareness. Clarity replaces confusion. Peace replaces uncertainty. I understand now. This is it.

Fragments of what I was told echo through me not in sequence, but all at once. "…Try imagining emptiness… no sound…no time… You simply are…and it simply is…" "Yes… this is what I am…but this is not easy for you to comprehend…" As the realization deepens, a thought forms: "This is what I was shown in the beginning…so why does it feel like the end? Is it because Alpha is Omega…and Omega is Alpha?" The moment that thought settles, something within me shifts. A new awareness is born. Then I hear it again: "Take note of what you witness. This will be the first of many times I allow you to see in this way…Now journey toward Eden…and prepare to open your eyes forward… You will become the narrator…speak as yourself…no one will silence your voice or your knowledge…Listen for your name. When you hear it again… restore your sight."

Instantly, the barrier releases my hand. The light intensifies as if the sun itself is rising behind my eyelids. I attempt to open my eyes…but something holds them closed. Then I remember. I've only heard my name once. So, I wait. I lower my hand and adjust my stance, balancing the woman on my shoulder. Suddenly, a surge of energy moves through me with excitement, urgency, purpose. “I remember!” I shout. “But what must I do to pass through this trial?” The response is immediate. “Push. Just push.”

Without hesitation, I reach forward again but before I can make contact, an overwhelming pressure crashes down onto my shoulders. The weight shifts. It’s no longer just her. It feels as though something far heavier has taken hold pressing me down from both sides. I can’t lift my arms. I can’t move. It feels like I’m being crushed…yet there’s no pain. “I can’t push,” I say aloud. “I can’t even move.” I’m not afraid but I am concerned. If I can’t move forward…how can I fulfill what I was meant to do? The light behind my eyes grows stronger brighter than ever.

Then, suddenly two voices speak at once. Perfectly synchronized. One is unmistakably Alpha. The other…is not. “You’re doing great. Try one more time…I promise” The voices merge…then separate. Only Alpha remains. “…Wajolebe.” At the sound of my name, I inhale sharply. My body reacts before I can think. I begin to open my eyes slowly fighting against the overwhelming brightness. And as I do… the two voices merge once more, completing the sentence: “…it will be…”

Chapter 8: To the End

The End.

Or perhaps… the beginning.

www.ingramcontent.com/pod-product-compliance
Lightning Source LLC
LaVergne TN
LVHW090522110826
845146LV00003B/947

* 9 7 9 8 9 9 5 9 3 6 4 0 4 *